A Man Among The Helpers

D1572060

Salvatore Gencarelle

with

Russ Reina, a firetender

"A Man Among the Helpers," by Salvatore Gencarelle. ISBN 978-1-60264-939-2 (softcover), 978-1-60264-940-8 (ebook).

Library of Congress number: 2012902969.

Manufactured in the United States of America.

Prayer of the Sacred Pipe

As Translated by Salvatore Gencarelle

Father Great Mystery, as I stand here I send my voice to you. I call out to you, even though I'm so far below you my voice may not reach you. I remember this creation you have made and say these words in thanksgiving.

I first remember all the beings of this world that you have made to live in the clouds, all the winged beings, from the skin of the sky to where the heavens meet the earth.

I remember all the beings that live and move upon the earth, and all the beings that live and move within the earth, and the beings that live and move in the waters, all the way to the very bottom of the waters.

These beings of the sky, earth, and water you have made for us to know you and to learn, and through your creation, to communicate to you.

Here now, as I stand, I also remember and give thanks to all the many types of trees, all the many types of fruit trees, all the many types of shrubs and bushes and herbs, all the many types of roots, and all the many types of grasses of this world. I remember these beings who provide for all our needs in this life; those who protect us, heal us, clothe us, feed us, warm us and all the many other ways not mentioned.

We natural humans and creatures live in this world you have made and it is good. This I remember as I stand here.

The Sun, the Moon, the Thunder Beings, and the Stone; as I stand here, I remember those that are forever sacred.

AUTHOR'S NOTES:

This book is my personal experience with the traditions of the Lakota people. I do not claim to be Lakota, nor an expert on all things Lakota. I can only speak from my times with these medicine ways and ancient traditions. Lakota spirituality is not a dogmatic religion; each medicine family has its own particular connection to the Grandfathers, and these various connections require different approaches. Due to this, what you read here may differ greatly from your own personal experiences or understandings of Lakota or other Native American traditions.

The orthography used in this book is mainly derived from the system used by the Oglala Lakota College. This system closely resembles the orthography used at other colleges, including Sinte Gleska College and the University of Minnesota, Minneapolis. The author's primary study of writing the Lakota language occurred while attending Lakota classes at the Oglala Lakota College.

Just a few weeks before this book was to be sent to the publishers, I was reminded of a teaching that the Grandfathers had spoken long ago. Over the years, I had often heard that this teaching was "the most important thing for people to know."

The teaching is this: *"If we use a tool on sacredness, we profane sacredness. The only way to make this right is for the person using the tool to maintain the highest level of prayer."*

The Grandfather's teaching about using tools gives us the information we need to know in how to conduct our everyday lives, to bring about the spiritual healing that is so critical now. This is no small statement. Consider it well.

For more information on what I'm currently working on, please feel free to check in with my website: www.manamongthehelpers.com or e-mail me at: sal@manamongthehelpers.com

Peace,

Salvatore Gencarelle

A FIRETENDER'S NOTE FROM RUSS REINA:

When I first met Sal, he was 18 and I, 45 years of age. We were on the Pine Ridge Indian Reservation in South Dakota. I was tending sweat lodge (Inipi) fires for the Chipps family, something that I did periodically through the 1990s. Sal had just started setting altar for Godfrey. That was 1991, and our lives intersected over ceremony on a number of times over the next nine years, usually in stretches of weeks at a time. In the summer of 1992, I tended fire for a couple of months straight for the Yuwipi ceremonies, working closely with Sal. I witnessed many of the things spoken about here.

It was then I realized that Sal was part of an enormous story; perhaps one of the greatest American stories of my lifetime. In the year 2000, we met again at a Sundance in Oregon. Since, Sal had married Godfrey's daughter, fathered children with her, and had been living on the "Rez" assisting Godfrey in ceremony. At that time I simply said, "When you're ready to tell your story, let me know."

In 2010, we both found each other again through Facebook. He was ready. But here's the thing: all the time I had known Sal and worked with him in ceremony, we had perhaps two conversations with each other! Only one of them—lasting just a few minutes—had anything to do with the amazing things we and everyone around us was experiencing. Being in service to Spirit was our common bond, though compared to him I was no more than a tourist. I got to see his entry into this unique world.

As I pursued my exploration of the healing arts, I periodically checked in to observe how he became part of this way of being, and how he followed its dictates to the letter, resulting in an incredibly intimate relationship with the ways, the family, the medicine and the life. Most importantly, I came to realize he, specifically, was being prepared to use what he was shown to be applied today and for future generations. I understand this process to be a continuation, much like the translation of an ancient spiritual understanding into a different language.

I approached this work as I do the Inipi. My role is to facilitate the prayers of the people by tending the fires of spirit that move through them. This is Sal's prayer for future generations, and I am humbled to have played a small part in it.

You can find my work in the healing arts through my primary website at www.firetender.org and I can be reached via 1firetender@gmail.com.

Table of Contents

INTRODUCTION

The year was 1989. Spiritual forces were at work, calling out to those who could hear. The damage to the world that humans had inflicted had just passed a critical point—the Earth could no longer be healed physically. A spiritual calling was being shouted from deep within the Earth for aid, and many people heard the call at this time. All over the world, contemporary humans turned to traditional indigenous people for help. Many began seeking to live a more balanced, spiritual life.

It was during this time that I unexpectedly received a great Vision—a Vision that changed my life and transformed me from a self-centered teenager into a healer. I embarked on a mission to learn what this calling meant, and what I needed to do. Within months I began helping a Native American Medicine family in sacred ceremonies. Within a few years, I was living with and had married into this family, one of the last direct links to ancient Native American medicine.

In that time of my youth, I set up the altar for sacred Lakota ceremonies. I worked with Benjamin Godfrey Chipps, a spiritual interpreter of the Oglala Lakota Sioux; a practitioner of the "Yuwipi" ceremony with blood links to its originator. I spent over 10 years being educated in traditional medicine and healing practices. Through this medicine, I learned the healing power of the Earth. I became a translator for the ceremonies, which are bridges linking the ancient Lakota way of life to the present moment.

Now the calling has brought me back into mainstream America. Over these past few years, I have come to understand better my purpose in learning these sacred ways, to help remind this modern

1

world of the sacred knowledge and the true meaning of health and happiness.

My story and the information contained in this book are based on my personal experience. This book describes Native American concepts, philosophies and actual ceremonies from a modern perspective. I was on outsider, raised in another culture but still welcomed with open arms into an ancient way of life. During my training, I was taught healing practices that can be traced back to the foundations of the Earth. I was expected to fully explain these concepts to non-native ceremonial participants. This book is a continuation of my responsibility to preserve these ancient ways for all of humankind. Within this text is a template for each person with the desire and heart to find his or her own Vision.

Walk with your heart and mind together as one, and the path will unfold before you.

CHAPTER 1 -THE EARLY YEARS

My very first memories are not visual. I remember feeling love and purpose, the love that brought me into this world and the caring I received growing up from infancy to childhood. I remember feeling a sense of security and peace when in the arms of my mother; the sense that this life was given to me to serve a greater purpose. I felt that life was a part of a grander destiny.

At the dawn of my visual memory, I recall the house my family lived in during those very early years—a small house with a big yard, where my five siblings and I played and grew.

I was a wild child, playing, running and usually doing everything and anything I wanted. If I felt like jumping out of a tree, I did. If I had an impulse to play on a road, then that's where I would be. I think I drove my mom crazy trying to keep up with me. I remember getting punished often, but getting away with much, much more.

It was during this time that I became conscious of responsibility. There is one particular early memory I have that made it clear we have a power within our minds that needs to be controlled. I was about six years old at the time.

I got in trouble again. What I had done, I'm not sure. My mother punished me this time by sending me to bed in the middle of the day. I was lying on my bunk bed feeling sorry for myself. The sun still was high in the sky, and I wanted to play outside, not be stuck in this stinky old room. Staring up at the bottom of the mattress of the top bunk bed, I felt immense anger well up in my chest. It became so intense that I wished for my parents to go away.

During this fit of self-pity I suddenly became aware of what I was thinking. It was as if I was standing outside of my own body,

3

looking back at myself for the first time, seeing who I was and the ugliness of what my mind could create.

In that moment, I stepped into a future created by those negative thoughts. My parents had died, and I saw the pain and suffering of my family. I watched as my siblings were scattered to relatives across the country; my sisters rebelling from abuse and being sent to foster homes, where life went from bad to unbearable, and my oldest brother going into a depression and never recovering, eventually becoming an alcoholic and dying young. Only my younger brother lived a peaceful life, not having memories of parents that had died when he was an infant.

I realized that this could easily be the future if the negative thoughts of my mind became reality. I saw how a horrible reality can be manifested by a mind out of control, unaware of its power and acting from ignorance and negativity. In that moment, I took heed of the warning I heard: "A person must control their desires, or they will be destroyed by them."

I believe the wisdom I gained at this moment was the first step in my becoming an adult. I realized that with each thought, wish or prayer, one should pause and ask these questions: "What are the potential consequences of this?" and "Is that what I really want?" This realization was just one part of becoming self-aware and responsible.

A year after my moment of consciousness, my parents sold their house in Massachusetts and began to wander around North America with my siblings and me. Their goal was to move to a better place to raise their children. As far as I knew, they had no destination, just a goal. We left our family and friends, and began a great adventure that gave us a unique view of American life.

Our travels took us coast to coast, through 48 states. We stopped at many historical markers and sites. We flowed from one "point of interest" to another. I truly enjoyed traveling all over, learning about history and cultures. We traveled for three months straight, never staying in one place more than a week.

The most unique part of our travels was that we didn't stay in a motel or camp out the way most people do. We lived in a tipi! My father had bought one a few years earlier and set it up in our backyard. It took a few days for him to get it up right, but when he finally got it standing in good order, it remained that way. I loved it the moment I saw it. I climbed the poles to sit in the crown and look out over town, or swung on the tie-down rope like it was my own personal playground.

Staying in a tipi is like no other camping experience. It is not a tent—it's a movable home. Living in one changes the way you see and feel about the world around you. Living in a circular room, close to the Earth, alters a person in dramatic ways.

The tipi, according to the legends later told to me, was a gift to the people from the Great Mystery, Wakan Tanka (wah-kan tan-kah). This gift was delivered to the people by the White Buffalo Calf Woman during a time of great need.

As the legend was told, White Buffalo Calf Woman came to the first people of this world. In those days, people were "new" upon the earth and not equipped for the hardships of the environment. The people didn't know how to live upon the Earth, and they were dying. At this time, they didn't even have livable homes.

The people cried out for help, and their call was answered. The White Buffalo Calf Woman came to the first people and instructed them on how to live in balance and harmony. Included in these teachings was the design of a special house, the first tipi. Through her teachings, she gave people the means to live and sustain themselves, both physically and spiritually.

Because the tipi was a gift from the White Buffalo Calf Woman, it is of perfect design. The tipi is constructed to withstand tornado-force winds, and provide warmth in sub-arctic temperatures and comfortable shade in 100-plus degree weather. It is suitable for an incredible number of different environments. This design spread across North America to many tribes. To me, living in a tipi is comparable to living in a church and sleeping at the foot of an altar.

The White Buffalo Calf Woman brought the first gifts to the people at a time when there was no separation between spirituality and daily life. They were viewed as one and the same. The tipi is both a secular home, and the home of the sacred. In that sense, my earliest experiences of sacredness happened in one of Wakan Tanka's first gifts to the people.

While living in the tipi, my young consciousness began to change. I began to feel more connected to the natural world. At night, lying close to the Earth, the warmth of the fire at the center comforted me. I'd watch the orange glow of the firelight flames dance on the walls. Through the smoke hole above, I could see the movement of the moon and stars. Looking at the spiral of poles and how they joined together at the center was very calming. Laying there, I could feel the spinning of the world around me and the very pulse of the Earth. Through the structure of the tipi, I knew my place in the circle.

After three months of traveling and living in the tipi, we eventually ended up in Minnesota. We moved to the shores of the Mississippi, to a town called Lake City. There we lived for five years. It was a small town, with small-town problems. I never felt at home there. My family and I were always considered outsiders. Maybe it was the tipi in our yard that put people off. Even the woods and the wilderness there felt unfriendly.

Often when my brothers or sisters and I were playing in the nearby forest, an eerie feeling would come over us, like someone or something was watching. Now that I know the history of that area, I believe what we felt was the negative energy left over from the Indian Wars that occurred there only one hundred years before. I was happy when we finally moved back to Massachusetts.

Due to economic conditions in the Midwest, we ended up moving to a town called Easthampton in Massachusetts, just one town away from where we had started our journey across America. It was nice to be back East. At this time, I had developed a passion for drawing and someday wanted to create great works of art. I truly cherished the act of creation and loved to draw. I felt that when I drew something, I somehow connected to it on a deeper level. I began to draw many things, but what I felt inspired to draw most were old black and white pictures of Native Americans. These old portraits fascinated me. The look in the eyes of the people spoke to me about forgotten knowledge and wisdom, something I began to yearn for.

Besides my interest in art, I was just a typical fifteen-year-old. I liked hanging out and skateboarding. I was attending the local high school and working in a nearby restaurant. I had a variety of friends, and we would often run around the city streets, getting into all sorts of mischief. I just wanted to have fun, make some money at my job, get good grades in school and keep my parents off my back. I really didn't feel like I had a purpose in life beyond my own wants and needs.

CHAPTER 2 - THE DAY MY LIFE CHANGED.

It was mid-summer of my 15th year. I had just finished work at a local seafood restaurant in the nearby town of Northampton, about four miles from home—a short ride on my 12-speed bike.

10 o'clock and Northampton was still lively, with people coming out of the movie theaters and enjoying the night at the local park. I quickly passed through the city, wondering which friends would be out running around and having fun, skateboarding or smoking cigarettes. I knew they would be talking and hanging out late into the night. Normally I would have stopped to visit, but I felt a gentle pull to go directly home that night. I followed my heart and traveled right to it without stopping.

I enjoyed the ride that night. There were few cars on the street, so I felt like I owned the road. Traveling at high speed made the air feel cool during the humid New England night. I laughed as I swerved back and forth across the road.

The city lights disappeared in a swish of air and pumping bike pedals. I entered into the darkness of the black-top road. The trees were calm, and a mist hung in the air, moist with the humidity of the day. I passed through pockets of warm and cooler air as the elevation of the road fluctuated. The only noise heard was the hum of my tires, my deep breathing, and a chorus of crickets singing as I sped through the darkness.

As I approached the edge of Easthampton, the city lights slowly became more visible, creating a red-yellow glow that illuminated the sky. Soon street lights were shining on the road. My journey home was almost at an end. I whipped into the driveway. I passed by the front of the house and noticed the blue glow from a television through the front window. I wondered who was watching T.V. so late as I parked my bike at the back door. Upon entering the house, I went to the kitchen, made a beeline to the refrigerator and gulped down cold milk straight from the carton. Sweat began to bead and run down my temples and forehead.

With my last gulp, I noticed the faint sounds of the T.V. coming from the front room. I entered the living room to find my mother curled up on the couch with her "one-a-day" cup of red wine. She glanced up to say "Hi, Sal," in the way she has so many times before. She was watching a show about Native American ceremonies.

My mother always had a strong interest in Native American subjects. She sat absorbed in the program. It looked interesting, so I lay down on the floor and stretched out, still catching my breath and cooling down from the bike ride.

On the television, there was a picture of a young man on the side of a hill in the prairie. A blanket was wrapped around him as wind blew his long hair over his shoulders. A narrator told a story of a ritual entailing a young man going out into the wilderness to fast and pray for days, seeking wisdom and understanding to help his people. The young man endures hardship and physical suffering to receive gifts from the Great Mystery that will benefit his tribe.

This sacrifice allows the young man to be considered an adult in his tribe, and is a way for him to contribute to the health of his society. By completing this task, the young man comes to better understand his place within the community and the world.

The narrator called this rite of passage a "Vision Quest." I immediately identified with these concepts and felt a strong desire to perform this ceremony. I wanted to find my place in society. I also wanted to know what my purpose in life was, and to have a deeper spiritual connection to the world. In that moment I knew, with every fiber of my being, that I would someday do a Vision Quest. I knew that someday I would make this sacrifice, and I would bring back wisdom, knowledge, and understanding from the spirit world to "my" people.

The show continued and switched to a Navajo sand-painting ceremony. It documented a story of a young boy who was sick, so his parents took him to a Medicine Man. As I watched the ceremony progress, I was amazed. The level of focus and intensity in what I saw touched me deeply. The seriousness was palpable, and I could literally see the intensity and focus of every action of the participants. I thought, "Someday I will be a part of ceremonies like this!"

It was then, lying on the floor of my parent's house, that it happened—like someone flipped a light switch in my brain. Suddenly my mind illuminated and expanded, reaching out through time and space. Forgotten knowledge was abruptly returned to me. I felt more connected to the world than I ever had before, like I was part of everything, and everything was a part of me. This new revelation of interconnectedness expanded my awareness instantly. My mind seemed to stretch around the world and touch everything in it. I became more than who I was moments ago.

It was as if my neurons had re-routed their connections and the folds of my brain bent into new shapes. Suddenly, everything became clear. I sensed there was more to life than the selfish comforts and wants of this 15-year-old kid. I saw my connection to the Earth, not as a boy going to school, working, skateboarding, and running around town; but as a child in the loving embrace of Mother Earth, a Mother that gave birth to me and provided me everything in this world.

I recognized the Sun pouring life upon the Earth and fathering me and all my ancestors, the moon watching over the children of the Earth, as a Grandmother, and the clouds bringing the rains to feed the children, like an older brother helping his siblings grow.

In just a matter of minutes, I went from an average teenage kid to something more. This new understanding of interconnectedness suddenly gave me a fresh perception of my place in the world. It filled me with both wonder and awe—but also a sense of overwhelming danger.

I suddenly and clearly saw the destruction that people were causing to the Earth. I realized with horror that humans were killing the world. Our descendants would be left with unimaginable hardship and pain, unless we changed our path of ruin. I finally understood the human interconnectedness with the Earth and all its inhabitants; like a spider's web that linking each being with the other. I saw that this "web of life" is very real and now very fragile, due to the actions of people. Through this "Vision" I heard the Earth calling for help.

It was then that I knew someday I would sacrifice for the good of all people and the world, by entering into the purity of wilderness and asking for help from the Creator. I intuitively knew that nature and the spirit would provide guidance and hope for the future of humankind.

Deep instinct told me that someday I would sit on the hill as the ancestors had, forgoing personal wants and needs to gain knowledge and understanding to help people to live in a healthy way. I was positive that this would happen. With every fiber of my body, heart, mind and soul, I wanted this more than anything else I had ever wanted.

A tremendous pull from deep within the Earth was guiding me toward this future. From that moment forth, my life has had one ultimate purpose — to bring knowledge and understanding from the Great Mystery to my relations, to benefit future generations.

CHAPTER 3 -THE CIRCLE AND THE SACRED PIPE

Over the next year, my heart, mind, and soul were bent toward one goal—to understand what these revelations meant. I spent every waking minute relearning my relationship to the world. My heart had a new feeling; a feeling of connectedness toward all things, like lines that spread out and touched everything. As this experience continued, I needed more and more to be in nature, surrounding myself with Wakan Tanka's creation.

I walked in the woods every chance I got. I slept in nature and often went to a nearby mountain to pray. While there, new impressions inundated my mind. When I saw a deer, there no longer was an animal; instead it was a sister or brother. When I walked in the woods, my relatives the trees shaded me. I felt more than their physical presence, I felt their very spirit and I heard their voices in my heart. A stone became a grandfather, and the sky above, the living spirit of the world. I began seeing everything in terms of relationships.

I now understood that everything ultimately is from the Earth. The earth in combination with the Sun created all forms of life. We are all connected in so many ways, I was amazed. I was wrapped in this understanding, swimming through a sea of life and seeing it with new eyes.

As I awoke from the long, secure slumber of my youth, my new dream became real. It was as if I was seeing the world for the first time with clear eyes and mind. I could clearly grasp the truth of a reality that had eluded me before.

Awakening in me were distant memories of a world in balance. There, people lived in harmony with the Earth and all of creation. This was a time when the human race honored and respected nature. Memories of the world before people became disconnected from the Earth flooded into my being, revealing a time of peace and true prosperity. This is a state of being that resides within each of us; a place we can still attain.

I continued to learn and search out new information. At this time, I was not sure what steps I should take, so I immersed myself in learning about nature and spirituality, in particular Native American spirituality. Much of this was done though books, but a good part of it was accomplished by praying in the wilderness. I began to spend more and more time in the woods. I separated myself from people. I quit hanging out with my old friends and distanced myself from my family. I didn't want any distractions to separate me from my quest.

As the days passed quickly, my heart and mind were set on learning as much as possible. During prayer and meditation in the woods, I would see in my mind's eye a river of light. This river contained all knowledge, all possibilities, and all truth. Through my heartfelt desire and prayer, I could look into and occasionally touch it, but never enter it. I felt if I swam in it, I would change completely. This was something I was not ready for, yet. I sensed that if this river was crossed, then my life would end. It was a sacred place in the spiritual universe that must be respected.

The days kept moving as the river flowed, and I wandered in the woods looking for more of the truth. I climbed a nearby mountain and sat in the rain; I burned in the sun and walked in the shade of the forest. I felt the energy of the plants reaching for the Sun. As I passed, the rocks watched me, like sentinels guarding the land. Their voices spoke deep and slow with the wisdom of the ages. Above all of us, the vastness of the clouds moved.

I began to ask and pray for help to understand what I needed to do next. Sunsets and sunrises became a special time for me to pray. I noticed that the birds sang their songs of prayer and thanksgiving during those hours, and I felt compelled to join them. Every free day, I would go up to the mountain before sunset and locate a place to pray; a nice, flat area with a good view. Taking a handful of tobacco, I would hold it up and say a prayer to the Creator and the powers of the world, asking for help in my task. I'd sprinkle tobacco in a circle around me and sit at its center for hours. Many times I watched the sun drop beyond the western treetops. I often remained in that spot until the night spread from the east, and stars twinkled above my head.

At times, I would try to awaken before dawn and ride my bike as quickly as possible to the mountain, racing up the steep inclines and searching for a place to view the rising sun. I had heard an old saying that when the sun first breaks the horizon, one could know the truth. This is what I was after. Unfortunately I would race to the top, all covered in sweat and out of breath, only to be too late, or to find clouds obscuring the view.

When I did finally see the sunrise, I noticed something. I found that I can look at the sun as it rises, but when the full circle breaks free of the horizon and shines in all its glory, it is blinding and too bright to look into directly. I came to realize the power of the complete circle.

The circle is the embodiment of the universe. In nature, objects try to take a circular shape. In the unseen world, spirit moves in a circular motion. I saw that the circle was one of the foundations of reality as we know it, like gravity or time. We are bound and held by the circle, we are wrapped in the loving arms of the circle, and we are both part of the circle and contained in it. Later, I would come to a deeper personal understanding of the circle in the form of a medicine wheel.

During this time of learning, I read every book I could find on Native American spirituality. The concepts I read that would have been of little interest, or completely misunderstood just weeks before, now made perfect sense to me. They resonated in my heart. Out of all the different things I learned, the understanding of the sacred pipe, also known as a "Peace Pipe," felt the closest to my heart. The sacred pipe is called a "Canupa" (cha-nu-pah) by the Lakota.

The idea that a sacred instrument could be made from special materials of the Earth, fashioned by the hands of man and filled with tobacco and prayers, made perfect sense to me. This was another ancient memory that came back into my mind. When I first learned about the Canupa, it was like seeing a place that I knew as a small child but hadn't visited for years. There was something incredibly familiar about it.

I felt such a strong pull towards the Canupa that I made one for myself. I purchased a piece of Catlinite, the special red stone used to make a Canupa, often called "Bloodstone." This stone is quarried in only one place in the world, western Minnesota. It symbolizes the blood of the people. I purchased the stone at a local pow-wow and used my father's tools to shape it into a large bowl. I then fashioned a wooden stem, which represents all life on upon the Earth. My first Canupa was complete. Now I just had to be taught how to use it.

At this time, I read the story of the White Buffalo Calf Woman and the coming of the first Canupa. Years later I was told a similar but more complete story about the Canupa by a Lakota Medicine Man. This is what I was told:

The Canupa came to humans back in the days when "the grandchildren were few." People were new to the Earth and did not know how to survive in this new environment. They were dying. People did not know sacredness, but they knew there were powers in this world. So they "sent a voice out," a prayer, to anything that would listen and respond to their cries for help.

An elder in the group had a dream. The people's cries for help had been heard. Help was coming. In this dream, the elder was instructed to send a young man into the wilderness to greet the help that was on its way. The elder told his dream to the people, and everyone gathered to hold a council. During the council, they chose the best young man in the camp to go to meet whatever was coming.

The young man was made ready and walked out into the wilderness. As he left, another young man snuck out of camp and came to walk beside the first. This sneaky one was bad and only sought to benefit from the situation. The good allowed the bad to travel with him into the wilderness as he looked for something, not knowing what.

After some time, they climbed a hill, where they could see out across the land. There they saw an object moving toward them, so they waited for it to come closer. As the object approached, they saw it was a beautiful young woman carrying a red bundle. Now, when the bad man saw this woman, he said they should rape her, because no one was around or would ever find out. The good one told this sneaky man to not say such things and to put those thoughts out of his mind, for she was "approaching in a mysterious manner."

Finally, the woman reached the men and set her bundle down upon dried buffalo dung. She told the bad man,"What is in your thoughts? Come do it."

The good young man watched his companion go to the woman. A mist formed and covered them both. From within the mist, a scream like a dying animal resounded. The mist cleared and the woman stood there, but all that was left of the bad man was his bones. When the good man saw this, he was afraid and began to run away.

The woman commanded him to stop. She instructed him to have the people build a house (tipi) with the door facing east, and that she would arrive at his camp when it was complete. She told him that she was bringing something for all the people.

The man returned to the camp and told all that had happened, and explained what the people were to do. Over the next days the tasks were completed, just as this woman had instructed. When the people were done, the woman appeared, coming from the east towards the tipi they built. As she walked, she stopped four times and raised the bundle she carried over her head. After the fourth pause, she entered.

The people would normally have offered her something to eat, but at this time there was nothing but water with sweet grass dipped in it. After she took the water, she held council and gave instructions to the people. She presented the Sacred Pipe to the people and explained how they were to use it to pray. She also provided instructions on how people were to live upon the Earth in balance and harmony.

Before she left, she gave this warning: "If you ever do away with the Canupa, then a nation will be no more."

After she completed her instructions, she exited the tipi and walked to the North. As she walked, she paused, and then wallowed in the dust four times. Upon the fourth time, she stood as a woman, and before the eyes of the people she turned into a buffalo calf and ran off to the North.

Just after the White Buffalo Calf Woman left, a man stepped forward. No one in camp knew this man or had ever seen him before. He also presented a gift to the people, the first bow and arrows. He then showed the people how to fashion bows and make arrows themselves. He taught them how to hunt and kill more efficiently.

From that day forth, as long as humans followed the White Buffalo Calf Woman's instructions, they flourished in harmony with the Earth.

The Sacred Pipe brought life, and the bow and arrows brought death. This is the balance.

CHAPTER 4 -MEDICINE WHEEL GARDEN

As this awakening was occurring in my life, my parents had met an herbalist at a local farmers market. His name was George and he owned a plot of land in the same town. Through my parents, George and I became friends. He took me under his wing and began to teach me the healing potential of plants. In exchange for his teaching, I helped him with his herb gardens and picked local wildflowers that he and his wife turned into bouquets.

As we worked, he explained to me the medicinal applications of the trees and plants we passed by. His understanding of herbal medicine was overwhelming at times. His connection to the Earth, nature, and spirituality seemed to be through his connection with plants. I tried to remember everything he told me during the time we spent working together.

It was during the summer of 1989, after I turned 16, that I began working on George's herb farm in Easthampton, a plot of land about five acres square. It had three old barns on it, one of which was remodeled into a house where George, his wife and their daughter resided. The land was tended in parts and overgrown with shrubs and grasses in other areas. It was very picturesque, and had a certain New England charm about it, with the little gardens and flower beds scattered around the property, and my prayer mountain off in the distance.

While my intention was to learn about herbs and natural medicine, my passion was more about the unseen power of things, rather than the physical. I believe George understood this better than I did at the time.

Early that summer, George told me about an idea he had for a Medicine Wheel herb garden. He explained this would be a place to celebrate and dance, and also a place of meditation and reflection. Not long after, he and I climbed to the top of an old barn on his property. It was a hot and humid New England morning. He pointed down to a treeless area of his property that was covered in chest-high grass, nettles and small bushes.

He began to describe his vision: "There will be an open area in the center, with gates to the cardinal and inter-cardinal directions." He pointed to the different areas and indicated every aspect of the design. His description was very detailed, but it was difficult to picture. I was thirsty, hot, and could only see a field that looked like tangled grass and thorny bushes. My only thought was, "This is going to be a lot of work."

We began working on the field immediately, and over time I came to understand the dedication needed in an undertaking like this. As the garden slowly formed, I gained a better appreciation for the energy it takes for a spiritual idea to be manifested physically.

Working on the Medicine Wheel was tedious and exhausting, but it became a labor of love. I felt alive in the act of creating this sacred garden. It was the same feeling I got when drawing a picture, but on a grander scale. George taught me about the "Zen of Raking," a meditation induced by repetitive motions. I found peace and contentment in working with the Earth. It was very satisfying.

Progress on the garden went more quickly than I expected, mainly because of George. To me, at 16 years old, George appeared aged, but his energy was boundless. In all the months I worked with him, I could never keep up with him. Even his walk was at a pace so quick that I would have to practically run to keep up.

The Medicine Wheel took shape, and before long the circle was cleared. I could finally see what George had been describing from the top of the old barn. Gates were formed with paths through mounded earth. Circles were shaped with shovels and rakes. The Medicine Wheel consisted of two circles. The inner circle was an open area, approximately 40 feet in diameter. The outer circle was a footpath that was divided from the inner area by a four-foot wide swath of mounded earth. The outer circle was surrounded by more raised earth. Entrance into the garden was through the inter-cardinal gates. Entrance into the inner circle was through gates posted at the cardinal directions. The raised mounds of earth were turned into plant and flower beds. The pathways and the inner circle were raked clean.

Soon, plants were set in their spots. I suggested planting corn, beans, and squash. I had heard that these plants were considered sacred foods to Native Americans, and I thought that a Medicine Wheel in North America should honor the native traditions. George had some very old Hopi blue corn that he planted on either side of the pathways.

When it was completed, the garden was truly a work of art. To this day I still marvel at the memory of it. Now I understand that this garden was a gateway into Native American spirituality for me, and for many other people. This Medicine Wheel garden was the first altar I ever helped make.

One sunny summer morning, I went to the farm to finish working on the garden. There was another project that George and I were working on as well, another garden, but this one was in the shape of the symbol of Western medicine. It was a caduceus; the serpents and the staff. When I arrived, I was anxious to get to work and looking forward to getting my hands in the dirt.

As I pulled my bicycle in to the driveway George met me outside his home with a big smile. He told me about a man who had stopped by earlier in the day. This man asked George about doing "purification ceremonies" at the farm. George mentioned something about a Native American Medicine Man. Even though he seemed excited, at the time I didn't think much of it. At the moment, I was focused on getting to work on the garden.

A few weeks later, George again met me in the driveway of the farm as I pulled in. He told me the man who had come by to talk about purification ceremonies was back, and he wanted to meet me. George had explained to him that I was the primary person who worked on the Medicine Wheel. Many aspects of the garden were created from my ideas. George had also explained my interest in Native American spirituality.

We walked inside to meet someone I now consider a true friend and mentor, Andy Cooksey. I found out later he was an adopted brother to Benjamin Godfrey Chipps, a Medicine Man of the Oglala Lakota, from the Pine Ridge Indian Reservation in South Dakota. Andy had lived on various Indian reservations off and on since the 1970s.

He had been under the guidance of John "Fire" Lame Deer. As Lame Deer saw his death approaching, he directed Andy to seek out Ellis Chipps to continue his education, since Ellis was one of the few "traditionals" who worked with white people. Ellis was the grandson of Woptura (wh-op-tur-ah), which translated to Chipps. Woptura and his children are credited with preserving the ceremonies through the darkest time of war and early reservation life. Lame Deer identified Woptura and his sons — one lineage named Chipps, the other Moves Camp — as the men who preserved the medicine ways of the Lakota during the worst of the "eradication" programs at the beginning of the 20th century.

Ellis Chipps, his wife Victoria, and their three sons, Charles, Philip and Godfrey, were keepers of these medicine traditions. Godfrey, it was said, inherited the powers of his Great-Grandfather Woptura, who is considered a Sacred Man by the Lakota — an "Immortal."

At this time, Andy was living at an East Indian meditation and yoga center in Massachusetts, not far from George's farm. Godfrey had recently called Andy and told him to look for a place to perform ceremonies. The Chipps family occasionally traveled for extended periods, doing healing ceremonies and teachings at various places around North America. During these times they would reach out to local contacts, like Andy, who would scout out a good location for them to do their work.

One day while Andy was searching for such a location, he passed by George's farm. Andy felt "pulled" toward the farm and immediately turned around. He spoke to George that day, a few weeks ago, explaining what he was looking for and why. Once Andy saw the Medicine Wheel garden, he knew it was what drew him to the farm, and he knew that it was the right place for the ceremonies.

That day, when I walked into George's normally quiet and peaceful house, I heard someone talking far louder than what I thought necessary. Andy was on the phone, talking to someone in South Dakota. I had barely sat down when Andy hung up, swung around in the chair and introduced himself with a jolly grin. He turned out to be a charismatic, friendly man in his 40s, with a head of almost pure white hair that trailed over his shoulders.

Andy had this excited energy about him that made everything seem very alive, and very important. He explained that there was a Sundance back "home" in South Dakota, and he was going to be leaving for it soon. This particular Sundance was in memory of his adopted father, Ellis Chipps, who had passed away earlier in the year.

Andy went on to explain that the Medicine Man, Godfrey, would be coming out to Massachusetts to do the purification ceremonies, but it would have to wait until after Sundance. Andy left for South Dakota that very day. I think George was just as excited as I was. Imagine, a real Medicine Man from the Lakota tribe doing a ceremony here at the farm!

In the weeks that followed, I continued to work on the garden. Eventually high school started again. It was my senior year. When I wasn't at school or working on the farm, I would still go to the nearby mountain or walk in the woods and pray. Finally, word came from Andy that Godfrey and his family would arrive in September.

CHAPTER 5 -MEETING THE MEDICINE MAN

The days dragged on until finally, September arrived. What started out as purification ceremonies eventually evolved into a public workshop. Word spread that Godfrey, his brother Charles, and his mother, "Grandma" Chipps, were coming to Massachusetts to hold Lakota ceremonies. The workshop included Native American teaching, praying, and a sweat lodge ceremony. It was scheduled for the fall equinox. Flyers went out, and people from all over New England began to sign up. Soon there were 30 people registered. The participants arrived at the farm at the time and date indicated on the flyer.

My introduction to "Indian time" happened then — Godfrey and his family didn't arrive until two days after the first scheduled day of the workshop. Indian time is a general term that basically means things will happen when they are supposed to. Most of the delays in their journey were due to cars breaking down. For many, that would be considered a very stressful event. However, when viewed through the eyes of Indian time, events like this are all just part of the Great Mystery. There is no stress, just an understanding that events unfold the way they are supposed to, all for the greater good. There is freedom in this way of thinking that creates a happier existence.

One day before the Chipps family arrived, Andy gathered all the participants together to drum up some more money. Andy explained that a vehicle had broken down again and needed repairs. Everyone at the meeting was sitting or standing in a circle, and one at a time, they stated what they would contribute. Some people said they could donate five dollars; others donated $100 or more. When it was my father's turn, he said he didn't have any money, but he could donate his second-born son, Sal, to the Chipps family. Everyone laughed, myself included.

It was during this time, before the Chipps arrived, that I first overheard talk about "selling the medicine." This was and continues to be a hot topic that everyone has an opinion about. I noticed that the discussion of money and payment for ceremonies generated very strong emotional responses.

Some people were happy to contribute, and were willing to do whatever it took to learn and participate. Others felt it was wrong for them to "pay" for ceremonies. They said that it wasn't "traditional" to be asked for money for anything related to ceremony. At the time, I wasn't sure how I felt about this. I did notice that the people who were more giving seemed to be more positive and happy, and the ones that refused to "pay" were very negative. One thing I was sure about was that everyone had to "pay" to go to the doctor, chiropractor or day spa, and most probably supported their various churches through donations as well.

Even then, I knew the cost of the workshop was minimal compared to what the participants could learn. For a two-day workshop, people were asked to contribute $75. The money they paid didn't even cover the cost of transportation and the daily needs of the Chipps family. Even the $75 was considered a donation, and no one was turned away due to his or her inability to contribute financially. What Godfrey and his family were offering to the people was far more valuable than money. Beyond just allowing non-natives an opportunity to attend a traditional purification ceremony, the Chipps family was also introducing people to an ancient way of life that could sustain them and their families for generations to come.

Andy explained that everyone in Godfrey's family is involved in teaching these ceremonial ways. In their culture, as members of a medicine family, everyone has a critical role to play. Each family member is a caretaker of the medicine as passed down by their ancestors. With their combined traditional knowledge and experience, they were providing teachings and healing on a level nearly impossible to find in this day and age. In exchange for passing on this sacred knowledge accumulated over many lifetimes, people were asked to give money from their hearts.

It was during this workshop I also noticed that some people had a misconception that money would buy them what they were looking for, spiritually or physically. There were some people at the workshop who truly believed money could buy them the "medicine." They had become so accustomed to money getting them whatever they wanted in life, they thought all it took to get anything was to pay cash for it.

As for me, I realized that money only provided the chance for a person to grow. A person still must squeeze every learning experience from that opportunity. The only way to truly get the benefits of any opportunity is to do the work and put in the time. Only then can a person incorporate this growth. Money can't buy wisdom.

Years later, I heard a comment from a Lakota healer that summed up the issues about giving money for ceremonies. He had just done a week of healing for many people. All the people that were restored to health had come to him sick and with many questions, but they left happy and knowing all they needed. Most of the people that were healed had given this man blankets and star quilts, and someone even gave him a buffalo robe, but no money. When the week was over and everyone had left, he was sitting in a meager room in his dilapidated house. He sat with his head hung low, exhausted from all the ceremonies of the past week. There were piles of blankets stacked about him. There in his house, with no gas in his car and no food on his table, he sadly said, "I can't eat blankets."

The workshop quickly approached, but the delays caused by the broken-down vehicles forced the start time back two days. A few of the attendees had to leave, but most stayed. The night of the Chipps family arrival, there was to be a potluck dinner at the farm.

The evening approached with much excitement. It turned out that Godfrey was the only one who would be coming to the potluck. Grandma and Charles had arrived late and were resting at a nearby motel. It was too bad they had to stay at the motel, but everyone felt honored to finally meet Godfrey.

My parents and I were among the last to arrive to the farm, because we had finished cooking our contribution late. The meal was in a large room of one of the vacant remodeled barns. A few chairs and tables of food were scattered about the room. As soon as we walked in, I noticed that everyone was standing in little groups, talking loudly, seeming to having a good time. While carrying in a dish, I noticed Andy and a Native American man, who I assumed to be Godfrey, standing off to the side of the room. In their silent isolation, they seemed uncomfortably out of place.

After setting down the dish I was carrying, I took a long look at Godfrey. He wore a black baseball cap, a leather jacket, blue jeans, and white high-top sneakers with the tongues sticking out. He was short and stocky. I really wasn't sure if this was the Medicine Man I had heard so much about. He had such an unassuming presence. I guess I really didn't have an expectation of what he should look or act like, but Godfrey wasn't anything like I imagined a "Medicine Man" to be.

It's not like I thought he would be wearing fringed leather and eagle feathers, or he would appear out of thin air with the clap of a thunderbolt, but this man standing there wearing a motorcycle jacket and white high-tops did not fit any of my preconceptions. As it turned out, Godfrey is something of a master at not conforming to anyone's preconceptions.

The dinner continued sociably. We all ate and chatted for a while. My father and Godfrey seemed to get along immediately. I stood off to the side and just listened, trying to absorb the whole experience. Before long, Godfrey said a few words to everyone about getting an early start tomorrow, and quietly exited. The feast ended shortly after he departed.

CHAPTER 6 -BUILDING THE SWEAT LODGE:
THE WOMEN'S SWEAT

The workshop got underway the next day. There was a big meeting, and Andy was its chief. Godfrey was nowhere to be seen. Seated together were about 20 to 30 people. The attendees ranged from wandering hippies to professionals seeking spirituality. Andy explained that we now had the opportunity to build a sweat lodge.

From Andy, we found out that the Lakota sweat lodge is the structure where purification ceremonies take place. It is made of fresh-cut saplings stuck in the Earth in a circle. These are then bent and wound together, and connected to form a dome. The saplings are tied with strips of cloth to hold them in place as they dry. It has one door that faces west, with a small altar of mounded earth a few feet from it. A "staff" is place on the west side of the altar. The staff is a straight tree or pole that stands about six feet high. Beyond the altar is the fire pit, used to heat the stones for the ceremonies.

Andy explained that before this day ended, we had to gather saplings, firewood, and forty melon-sized stones, dig a fire pit, make an altar, and assemble the sweat lodge. This workshop was going to be very hands-on.

As soon as the meeting ended, many people began ambling about the farm like they were lost, clearly avoiding work. This was the first time, but not the last, that I witnessed people asking to learn, but unwilling to work for the knowledge. I noticed then that often the people claiming to be the most spiritually enlightened were the most unwilling to actually do any type of physical labor.

Andy finally corralled enough people, and we set off to find the saplings that would form the structure of the sweat lodge. We ended up in a forested area on a piece of property owned by a friend of one of the participants.

The owner of the land was an old woman who walked with a cane. I heard someone say she was sick and dying. She lived in a cabin by herself, and she reminded me of a witch. Not a bad witch, just an old woman that you wouldn't want to have trouble with. She guided us to a tree not far from her cabin. It was the biggest tree I had ever seen! Here was an ancient tree that somehow had managed not to get cut down for hundreds of years. A branch had broken off, and this branch was as big as the trunks of the biggest trees for miles around.

The tree was dying. The thought came into my mind that this old woman and the tree's life were somehow connected, and that they were both going to die together. I could see the old woman truly loved trees, and they loved her.

Godfrey met us there. He pulled up to the cabin just as we walked into the woods. Standing next to the ancient tree, he said something to Andy in the Lakota language. Andy took a handful of tobacco and, holding it above his head, he prayed to the four directions. He placed this offering into a hole at the base of the tree. The old woman eyed Andy and Godfrey. Satisfied with the offering, she nodded her head and pointed off into the woods, towards the direction where we were to cut the saplings. As the group walked off deeper into the woods, I watched her slowly limp back to her cabin, supported by her cane.

Back at the farm, a handful of people had been left behind to prepare the site for the sweat lodge. Godfrey's brother, Charles, who I hadn't met yet, was supervising at first. The site selected for the lodge was at the Medicine Wheel garden. The sweat lodge structure was to be built on the east side of the garden, facing the center. A fire pit to heat the stones would be dug at the very center of the garden.

Progress on the site went quickly, until it came time to figure out the placement of the holes that would anchor the saplings in the ground. None of the people attending the workshop had ever built a sweat lodge, and Charles was either not helping or wasn't asked.

A discussion of how to best place the holes began. Soon, calculators were pulled out and tape measures were extended. The engineers present started to divide the circumference of pi. They kept making marks in the dirt, only to erase them and start over. This went on for quite a while and was still in progress when we returned with the saplings. When I saw what was happening, I wondered how the old Native Americans figured it out.

Andy finally stepped forward, looked at the circle and began making marks—here...here...here; just "eyeballing" the locations.

None too soon, the lodge finally took shape and was ready for use. Another group of people had gathered wood and stones. These were placed in a newly dug fire pit at the center of the garden. The fire was ceremonially stacked and ignited. As the fire burned, most of the attendees retreated to my parents' tipi, which had been erected near the outside edge of the Medicine Wheel. A few of the participants had been asked specifically to help tend the fire. The rest of the people at the tipi entertained themselves with discussions about spirituality and their personal experiences.

Two men stayed at the Medicine Wheel to be "fire tenders." They were responsible for ensuring that the stones were heated thoroughly and evenly. These men were in charge of not only the physical preparations, but also the spiritual. While tending the fire, there was very little conversation, if any. Every ounce of energy was expended in prayers for the ceremony to come. The fire had to be maintained with constant prayer and vigilance. If even one coal fell outside the circle of fire, the men would push it back into the burning pile. At no time were the "stone people" allowed to become uncovered. In this way, the fire tenders maintained the spiritual and physical integrity of the preparations.

After a few hours, the fire tenders sent word that the stone were ready, and the women would be sweating first.

Normally Godfrey's mother, Grandma Victoria Chipps, would lead the woman's sweat lodge. Grandma was the matriarch of the Chipps family. When she was a young woman, she had been recruited into ceremony life while living on the Rosebud Reservation. Grandma had been involved with the Episcopal Church and was responsible for preparing the altar at her local church. Horn Chipps, Godfrey's grandfather, being a powerful Medicine Man, saw her faith and level of belief and asked her to help with ceremonies.

Her main job in ceremony was to pray with the Canupa. To the Lakota, this is an incredible honor to bestow on a woman, and it speaks highly of her character. It is a difficult responsibility, a task not to be taken lightly. Grandma became an integral part of Horn Chipps' ceremonies and prayed with love for all. Eventually she met Horn Chipps' son, Ellis (Grandpa), and they married.

From this union, they had three sons: Charles, Philip and Godfrey. Grandma was blessed and was considered a medicine woman in her own right. She was so full of knowledge and wisdom that even her own children honored her by calling her Grandma.

Grandma was not available to lead the lodge that night, so Andy selected one of the female participants to pour water. We men remained in the tipi, waiting for our turn to sweat. I'm not sure what occurred in the women's lodge, but suddenly we heard loud crying and wailing from inside the lodge.

I later found out that the woman pouring the water began to talk about the abuse women suffer and encouraged them all to cry, very loudly. The lamentation arising from within the lodge did not seem appropriate to me. It sounded like the women were trying to force themselves to cry. After the sweat, some of the women stated that they also felt uncomfortable with the loud crying.

I understood that the sweat lodge is for purification, and sometimes crying would be a part of the process, but this wailing was something else — almost like anger. To me, a sweat lodge is a about celebrating life, and not a place to focus on negative thoughts.

CHAPTER 7 -THE MEN'S SWEAT LODGE

Finally, close to midnight, the fire tenders called for the men to gather at the lodge. Godfrey had already left for the night, so it fell to Charles to lead the ceremony. The men were instructed to undress and cover up with a towel. It was a chilly autumn night, and the moon was almost full. The air was refreshing. Charles was the first to enter the lodge, bowing low and saying, "Mitakuye Oyasin" (me-ta-koo-yea o-yah-sin), which roughly means "All My Relations." Once he was seated, the rest of us came in single file, each saying the prayer of All My Relations as we entered.

Lakota is a difficult language to effectively translate into English. Behind Lakota words, there is a culture, history, and spiritual version of the world that is very different from the background of the English language. Lakota words, like all words, are verbal expressions of ideas. To translate Mitakuye Oyasin into the words "All My Relations" really does not convey the idea. A more accurate translation would be something like this: "I recognize that I am connected to all things, and all things are my relatives; I will approach all aspects of life in this manner." This is why Mitakuye Oyasin is an often-repeated prayer. It mentally and spiritually reinforces our interconnectedness, and reminds us of our place within the universe.

After someone says "Mitakuye Oyasin," the men often say "Hau," which means they agree. This reinforces the idea that they are also related.

When all the men were seated, there were perhaps 15 people total. We sat in a circle around a shallow pit at the center of the lodge. Charles was sitting to one side of the doorway and Andy was sitting at the other side, assisting Charles. Andy called out to the fire tenders, instructing them to bring in the stones one at a time.

The stones were carried on a pitchfork to the entryway of the lodge. Andy then took the stones and placed them in the pit at the center, moving the rocks with deer antlers. The first five stones were greeted with silent prayer. One at a time, they were placed at each of the cardinal directions—west, north, east and south. The fifth stone was placed in the center of the first four.

As each stone was placed, a pinch of cedar needles was sprinkled on it. The stones were slightly larger than melons and had been in the fire for at least four hours. They were so hot, they glowed red. As soon as the cedar needles touched the stones, smoke began to billow. The smoke had a pleasant and familiar smell. After the fifth stone was placed in the center of the pit, Charles then said Mitakuye Oyasin.

An additional 25 stones were brought from the fire. The combination of the glowing red stones, the heat, and cedar smoke was intense. The red glow of the rocks produced enough light that I could see the faces of the people sitting across from me. Everything had a beautiful red glow to it. The combination of all the elements was quite mystical.

Charles called for the door to be closed. He began to speak about the creation of the Earth. Sitting there in the circle of men, looking at the glowing stones, it was like we were witnessing the newly formed Earth which had yet to cool. Seeing the rocks, feeling the heat, and hearing Charles speak of the beginning of the world, it felt like we were the ancient spirits, watching the Earth form. There we sat, as if waiting for this world to cool so we, too, could become physical beings.

Charles began to pour water on the hot stones. The water instantly turned to steam as it came into contact with the super-heated surfaces. We were already sweating, but the steam intensified the heat exponentially. With each dipper full of water, Charles would say a prayer. Some of the prayers were in Lakota, while parts of others were English. Waves of hot steam rolled over our faces and bodies. The steam opened our pores, and sweat dripped from us. The heat continued to build until I could hardly breathe. Finally,

Charles called for the "doorkeeper" stationed outside the lodge to open the door.

Cool air rushed into the lodge, mixing with the heat and steam. A solid fog formed instantly, and visibility inside the lodge was zero. Andy passed water out to the participants. Each got a full dipper to drink. The break from the heat both refreshed and re-hydrated us. Before we cooled off too much, the door was closed. Again, the process was repeated. Prayers, steam, and heat, and the door opened. This occurred four times. With each "door," the stones cooled a little more, and by the fourth door their heat had dissipated.

Charles then exited the lodge, again saying Mitakuye Oyasin. The rest of us followed in order. As we exited the lodge, most of the men collapsed to the ground on their towels. Some were unable to stand and just kept crawling. Visibly steaming bodies were sprawled all about the Medicine Wheel.

Charles and Andy were the only ones who did not seem affected by the heat. I thought to myself that they must be used to this, from years of sweating. I personally felt like I had just run a marathon. My head was spinning, and my heart pounded. Even though the night air was cold, I was still hot and sweaty. I lay down and watched the stars wheel in the sky above. I was happy.

The workshop concluded the next day with a Pipe ceremony. Many of the people that attended the workshop would later do more ceremonies with Godfrey. Most of the people left for now, but a handful stayed.

It was then I found out that there was to be a "healing ceremony" for a middle-aged woman with multiple sclerosis.

Andy knew this woman; they had met at the yoga center. She was one of the main reasons Godfrey had come to Massachusetts. She needed a healing and was willing to do what it took live a healthy life. The disease had progressed to the point where she relied on the support of a walker to get around. When she became tired, she could hardly move at all. She had exhausted all standard and alternative medical options available to her. She wanted to live, and now having nowhere else to turn, she looked to a Lakota Medicine Man for a healing.

CHAPTER 8 - A YUWIPI

Over the next few days, Grandma and Andy began to teach everyone who was going to attend the ceremony about the various offerings and the methods of prayer the Lakota use. We learned more about what the Lakota call the "Tunkasila" (tun-kah-she-la), which means Beloved Grandfather. Grandma explained that we pray to the Grandfathers, the spirit helpers and protectors of this world, and in turn they pray to Wakan Tanka, the Great Mystery, for us. Andy and Grandma showed us how to make tobacco ties and prayer flags.

Tobacco ties are small pinches of tobacco placed into cotton material while praying. This little bundle is tied with string and offered to the Grandfathers in exchange for what we ask. The prayer flags are similar, but larger, and the material hangs like a flag. These are tied to sticks from fruit trees.

Within Lakota spirituality, there is a strong sense of balance. Part of maintaining this balance is the belief that one should not ask for something without giving something.

Grandma often said that the prayer ties in Lakota spirituality are the equivalent of a Rosary to a Catholic. The tobacco, the material, the string, and all the other items used are just physical items. What makes tobacco ties a sacred gift are the prayers instilled in them by the people.

Every item offered to the Grandfathers has to be made and handled with focused intent, directed toward the sponsor of the ceremony. In this way, the energy of healing becomes stronger and builds up to the culmination of the ceremony.

The Lakota word for a healing ceremony is "Yuwipi" (you-we-pea). This means to be bound or tied. Yuwipi refers to the Medicine Man, as part of the ceremony, having his hands tied behind his back and being completely covered by a blanket, which is then secured with a rope, tied in a spiral around his body. His immobilized body is placed face down on a bed of sage in front of an altar. In a sense, the Medicine Man becomes a living offering. He is wrapped and tied almost exactly the same way the tobacco offerings are.

It was for this first ceremony that my father and a few other people were asked to be "Helpers." A Helper's job is to assist the Medicine Man in the preparations of the ceremonies. Often, when Godfrey traveled, he would select people he deemed competent and worthy to be trained as Helpers. This is both an honor and an immense responsibility. The task of preparing a ceremony is far too great for any one person; it often takes up to four or more people.

Due to time constraints, people who are selected as Helpers get a crash course in Lakota spirituality and culture. Usually the Helpers are told the physical aspects of the ceremony. It is expected that the spiritual understanding will come later.

Helpers are selected mainly based on their faith and their willingness to learn. I was not asked directly to help, but I started to help tend the sweat fires and assist where I could. I would often stand off to the side while people were receiving instruction, eavesdropping and learning all I could.

I found out my father was to aid in preparing the "Hocoka" (ho-cho-kah), or sacred space. The Hocoka is the combination of all the offerings made by the sponsor and participants. Included in the Hocoka are the altar, the tobacco ties and prayer flags, food for a feast, the bed of sage, and other assorted sacred objects. These items are arranged in a precise order and fashion, and each part represents an aspect of the world and universe.

The offerings of the tobacco ties, flags, and food have to be made or prepared the day of the ceremony. Before being used in ceremony, the items are purified by steam from hot rocks and the smoke of cedar. They then are arranged in the Hocoka in a very special order, with constant prayer. It is considered a mistake if any item is placed out of order, or if the Helpers don't maintain the highest level of prayer while preparing the Hocoka. Helpers are the hands of the Medicine Man and take care of all parts of the preparations that he cannot.

The Helpers received their instructions, and then Godfrey advised us he was going to remain at the motel during the day. The Helpers and Andy were now responsible for coordinating the preparations. Godfrey would come back to the farm when everything was ready.

The work of preparing for ceremony began early in the morning. The sponsor and her close family and friends, also known as "supporters," greeted the rising sun with a prayer, and then started the meticulous task of making tobacco ties.

Before making the tobacco offerings, the area had to be purified with "smudge." Smudge is the incense smoke of sweet grass or cedar. After the room was smudged, the tobacco ties were made by taking a one-inch square piece of cloth and placing a pinch of tobacco into the center. The cloth square was then folded so the material formed a small "bundle" of tobacco. This little bundle was tied with a half hitch loop and the string pulled tightly to ensure the bundle was secure. This was repeated until a continuous string of 405 ties was assembled, a line about 40 feet long.

The people making the tobacco ties and food offerings were instructed not to talk to each other unnecessarily, and not to be distracted from their prayers. While people made the ties, they were to attain and sustain the utmost level of prayer possible. Their prayers had to be continuous and only for the purpose of the ceremony. Tobacco ties are a physical expression of our prayers, and a gift in exchange for what is being asked. They are a powerful offering to the Grandfathers.

The woman with MS and her supporters also made four prayer flags. These are made in the same fashion that the ties are, only using more tobacco and larger pieces of material. Representing each of the four primary directions, they are made of natural material that is dyed black, red, yellow, and white. The flags are then tied to sticks from a fruit-bearing tree. The flags are used to mark the outer boundaries of the Hocoka in the ceremony.

The food was the last to be prepared. It has to be made without tasting or spilling. It also has to be made in constant prayer. This is the sacrament for the ceremony. All of the offerings are given to the Grandfathers as a gift, in exchange for the healing that they are being asked to provide. During the ceremony, the Grandfathers take a little bit of the food and at the same time bless it, making it both sacred and a form of powerful medicine. Even though the food is considered an offering to the Grandfathers, it is consumed by the human participants at the end of the ceremony.

Grandma elucidated the importance that once the material, string, tobacco and food have been gathered with the intentions of offering it to the Grandfathers, the items have to be handled with prayer and respect. Respect in the Lakota way is that they should not be stepped on or over, used for other purposes, or come into contact with women on their menses.

At the time, I could barely deduce why women on their menses were not allowed to participate in ceremony or be around ceremonial items. The Lakota call a woman's menses her "Moon Time." This is a reference to a woman's cycle being similar and deeply connected to the 28-day lunar cycle. It seemed like there was confusion about this subject, even among the Lakota. Later I came to a better understanding of this very special and powerful time in the lives of women. A woman's Moon Time is a gift of purification and a ceremony unto itself, and should not be mixed with other ceremonies.

What I was learning at this time was that things were done the way they were done, and with little or no variance. There is a protocol to ceremonies that has to be carefully followed. Sometimes, no deeper explanation was given.

A room in one of the remodeled barns at George's farm was selected to hold the ceremony. This was a large room, big enough to accommodate all who were to attend, with a central space large enough for the Medicine Man to be bound and laid down. All furniture was cleared and any external light sources were covered. The inside of the windows were completely covered with opaque plastic and secured tightly to the wall with tape. The room had to be completely "light-tight," even at midday, without a ray of sunshine from any source allowed to come in. Cushions were placed on the floor for the people to sit on during the ceremony.

The preparations were complete, and the nighttime hour when the healing was to take place approached fast. After both the men and the women had completed their purification sweat lodges, the people began to slowly gather near the ceremony room. I remained at the fire. Andy left and went to pick Godfrey up at the motel. We all waited anxiously.

Evening became night, and the night was wearing on when Andy finally returned. Godfrey was not coming. Andy told everyone that the ceremony was canceled, and we would do it tomorrow. We had to eat the food and let the tobacco offerings sit out overnight, and then burn them in the sweat lodge fire the next day. New food and tobacco offerings had to be made tomorrow. I felt let down by this news, but I understood that something or someone was not ready, though what it was, I did not know.

The ceremony ended up being canceled three days in a row.

Each day the preparations started the same way, with everyone hustling and bustling around the farm. By the end of the day, Andy would come from Godfrey's motel and say "things aren't ready yet" or "it's not time." I saw a lot of frustration and confusion in the participants. The woman with MS became weaker and more stressed. I believe some people doubted that the ceremony would happen at all.

Finally, on the fourth night, Godfrey appeared. The preparations had just been completed, after everyone purified in the sweat lodge. The anticipation and energy increased as we finally entered the ceremony room. A Helper was burning cedar and pouring water into a metal bucket filled with hot rocks at the doorway. As we entered the room, we stepped though a cloud of purifying smoke and steam. The room was illuminated by a single kerosene lamp. As soon as I stepped through the doorway, I could feel a difference in the energy. There was electricity in the air, and my ears began to ring.

We were instructed to sit, with men on one side of the room and women on the other. The cushions indicated where. The woman being healed had to be carried in by four of her male supporters. She had become so exhausted over the past days that she could no longer support her own weight, even with a walker. Once everyone was settled, the Hocoka and altar were created.

The last person to enter the room was Godfrey. He carried in an old leather suitcase with him. He set it in the center of the room, near to where Charles was seated. In it were all the "Sacreds," the consecrated instruments of healing used during ceremony. This included eagle feathers, eagle bone whistles, soil from their home on the reservation, rattles, and many other sacred tools. Most of the objects were carefully wrapped in red cloth.

Charles began setting up the central altar. He first placed the altar board on the floor. This is a 2x2 foot piece of plywood with holes drilled in it to hold the prayer flags. He then placed the sacred items on the board in special order. Charles unwrapped each item, gently passed it through cedar smoke, and then set it in place on the altar. This was a long, meticulous process.

My father sat next to Charles and kept cedar burning to use as smudge. Each sacred item was bathed in purifying smoke before it was placed on the altar. Another Helper was arranging the outer prayer flags and tobacco ties. The prayer flags that were attached to the sticks were placed into coffee cans filled with dirt. These were arranged to make the outside border of the Hocoka. After this, a Helper strung the ball of 405 tobacco ties from prayer flag to prayer flag, leaving the section from the yellow flag to the white flag open. This opening served as a gate for Charles, Godfrey and the Helpers to enter and exit. The entire Hocoka was about a 10x10 foot square. Within this area, Charles continued to arrange the altar. The food was placed along the east side in a line, very close to the tobacco ties.

At this time I closed my eyes to focus on my prayers. As I sat there, I began to see visions in my mind's eye.

From the infinite, I saw the world coalesce from space dust. The swirling matter slowly spun together, brought together by love, and the desire for life. The glowing ball of heat and energy slowly cooled, and soon became the Earth as we know it. Water formed from a pure energy and was wrapped around the stone. As water and the hot Earth mixed, steaming hot vapors formed the atmosphere and the sky. Different forms of life took shape within the water, the sky, and upon and within the Earth.

I saw plants shooting up and animals taking physical form. Then came the humans. I watched as mankind began to separate themselves from the animal nations. I saw humans living in caves and using fire to warm themselves. Then I witnessed as people began to manipulate the fire and the knowledge within. People began to make tools out of the very rocks they stood upon. Soon they spread across the world, and began changing everything.

Suddenly my mind shot back to the present. I realized that Charles and the Helpers were done setting up the altar. The ceremony was soon to begin.

Charles said the word "Hoka," and Godfrey burst into song from the back of the room. Godfrey's deep, raspy voice reverberated off the walls of the room, and the drumbeat pounded to the rhythm of our hearts. Charles' hands began to move, holding out offerings to each direction one at a time, and then placing each offering onto the newly completed altar. The song continued, and I watched him load a Canupa. As the song ended, the Canupa was passed through the cedar smoke. Charles then exited the inner area, walked clockwise around the room and handed the Canupa to Grandma, who promptly said, "Wopila!" (woh-pee-lah), meaning "I'm grateful."

Godfrey stepped forward, standing at the opening to the Hocoka with no shirt, shoes or socks on, only his blue jeans. His hair hung about his shoulders instead of being bound up in his typical pony tail. He turned and faced away from the altar, placing his hands behind his back. Charles and the Helpers began to bind his fingers with rope made of sinew. As Godfrey's hands were being bound, he began to say a prayer in Lakota. Next, a blanket was placed over his head and body. This was tied with a leather rope that was wound around both the blanket and Godfrey.

He then began to sing a muffled song from beneath the blanket as he turned to face the altar. The Helpers and Charles supported him as he wobbled there, bound and putting his faith in others not to let him fall. Once he faced the altar, he began leaning forward, supported by the Helpers. They slowly lowered him to the ground, until he lay prone, with his head toward the altar.

After Godfrey had been laid down on the bed of sage, Charles and the others immediately left the Hocoka and quickly sat down. The last man to leave the area strung the remaining tobacco ties across the opening between the yellow and white flag. Now, the string of

405 prayer ties delineated the border of the Hocoka, acting as a fragile physical barrier between the people in the room and the sacred space in its center.

Charles spoke quickly, reminding everyone that once the lights were extinguished, no one was to move from their seat. The lamplight was blown out and a Lakota song began. The drumbeat pounded out a steady, rapid rhythm.

The power of the song and drum seemed to reach out and inspire everyone in the room to join in. Our hearts beat together as one, and our voices raised a call to the heavens. My sense of the physical room dissolved away, replaced by a deepening sense of vastness all around us. Out of this space, a loud, piercing whistle sounded above where Godfrey was laying. As the whistle pierced the air, rattles began to shake to the beat of the drum. The rattling sounds flew about the room. I actually heard them hitting the walls and ceiling, bouncing off and then careening around the room again. The ceiling of this particular room was at least 10 feet high.

The energy in the room began to crackle. Tiny sparks of lightning began to appear from where the rattles' sounds emanated. The hairs on my arms stood up. We were all becoming charged with this incredible energy.

The song stopped and the rattles ceased their sounds, dropping to the floor. From the center of the room, Godfrey's muffled voice called out for the woman to pray. The lady with MS said a heartfelt prayer and begged for health. Grandma and Charles said prayers in Lakota.

The songs resumed. There seemed to be a lot of activity near the women. Sparkling rattles shook, and the whistle sounded. I felt a breeze move across my skin and rustle my hair. In the distance, I could hear Grandma continuously praying.

Then the song changed. A new song began with a different beat, like the thump of a heartbeat. The energy in the room felt like a celebration. Everyone in the room spontaneously burst into song, trying their best to sing the Lakota words. With a swish of air and the final rap of the drum, the chorus ended.

Godfrey began to speak from the center of the dark room. His voice was no longer muffled. but clear. From the sound and direction, I could tell he was sitting upright now. He spoke many words in Lakota, and ended by saying "Ho hecetu welo" (ho hey-chey-too way-lo), "it is so." At this point, everyone in the room was given a chance to voice their prayers, which many people did, praying for the health and happiness of the sponsor.

After the final song, the lamp was re-ignited. Godfrey was sitting on the bed of sage, and he was completely unwrapped from the blanket and rope. The perimeter of prayer ties was absolutely undisturbed.

I found out later that the Grandfathers untie Godfrey and give the blanket to one of the participants in the room. This is a type of healing for that person. As Godfrey later said, "Human hands tie me up, but it's the Grandfathers who untie me; it is the Grandfathers who are the last to touch this blanket, and their energy heals." Charles had received the blanket this night. As is usually practiced, he tossed it back to his brother in the center of the room.

Grandma, who was holding the Canupa and praying with it during the entire ceremony, took out a lighter, lit it, and began to smoke. She took a couple of long puffs, said "Mitakuye Oyasin," and passed it to the next woman. The Canupa continued to be smoked and passed around the room until it ended with the last man, who ensured it was completely smoked. It then was handed to Godfrey, who sprinkled some of the ash from the bowl onto the altar.

An offering of food was then placed on the altar. This consisted of a small pinch of bread that was smudged and offered to the four directions, the heavens and the Earth. After this, the Hocoka was taken down.

During the ceremony, the Grandfathers touch and bless the food. This food is no longer considered regular sustenance, it is now medicine. Everyone must take part of each item; no one should refuse any item provided in the feast. The first plate was set aside for departed loved ones. It is known as the "spirit plate." The Helpers then served out the food to the participants.

As I sat there eating the food, I felt great. I felt better and more content than I had for many years. Everyone was very relaxed, yet so alive. The intensity of the energy in the room had diminished, but we all were still feeling "buzzed."

The lady who received the healing then spoke. She asked Godfrey if she could give him a hug. Godfrey said, "Sure." He stood to walk to where she was seated. And she, who just an hour ago had to be carried in to the sacred ceremony, practically sprung up, strode across the room and gave him a hug.

There was an audible gasp from everyone in the room. We had just witnessed a miracle!

It was then that I knew my prayers for a teacher had been answered. This Medicine Man was the one who had been sent to me. I felt truly humbled and blessed, and I still do, even to this day.

CHAPTER 9 - THE VISION BECOMES REAL

Soon after the Yuwipi ceremony, Godfrey and his family went back to South Dakota. They had completed what they set out to do. The Chipps family loaded up their cars and were down the road in no time. It was sad to see them leave, yet this experience was so profound that it was going to take everyone a long time to process it. Suddenly, our world had expanded faster than it ever had before.

Just one day ago, we all believed that there was something very powerful and good in the world; unseen forces that helped us in our everyday life. Now we were sure of it. We had seen the power at work with our own eyes. All of the people that participated in ceremony that night were changed, and to this day are living new lives. Many of those participants continue to pray, make tobacco ties, Sundance and Vision Quest all across the country. These ways still live among us.

As for myself, I had found what I was looking for. I had confirmation of the thoughts and ideas that had been pouring through my head over the past months. At times over the previous months, I thought that I might have been going a little crazy. I occasionally had doubts about what was happening with me. Maybe I was just making this stuff up. Was I was living in a dream world that I had created?

But now I knew. I had confirmation that the powers are real, and still can be just as active in our lives as they were in the ancient stories. This experience opened up new doors that I never realized were there. As Godfrey had said during one of his teachings, "I am the Grandfathers' janitor; I just wipe the window clean, so you can see through it for yourself."

I saw through the window, and now could see that the door was open. The next step was to walk through the doorway myself.

CHAPTER 10 -PRAYING WITH THE CANUPA

I returned to high school. My senior year had already started, and I had missed quite a few days, but luckily the principal was willing to work with me. I made up my time and did extra homework. The days passed quickly, and my free time was occupied with thinking about my experiences with the Chipps family. During this time, I celebrated my 17th birthday.

I came to see that this spiritual path represented thousands of years of accumulated knowledge so incredibly powerful that even I, who had almost no inkling of Lakota history, culture, or thinking, could grasp it—and perhaps most astounding of all, utilize it. I fully realized that even in our modern lifestyle, we still possess our connections to the Earth and Spirit deep in our consciousness.

I picked up my Canupa and began using this sacred tool to gain a better understanding. During the purification workshop, Godfrey had blessed the Canupa, the one I made before we met. I began to use it as I had been instructed. I loaded the pipe with prayers to Wakan Tanka and to the Grandfathers of the six directions, praying for health and happiness for all of creation. I also prayed with the desire to be taught the deeper meanings of what the Chipps family had shared with me. Through the Canupa, I was assisted in remembering, embracing, and expanding upon those first lessons.

The first thing that I had been taught was that there are different ways to purify. The simplest method to purify an area, sacred items, or yourself is to smudge. This is done by burning cedar branches or sweet grass and allowing the smoke to scent objects and the room, similar to the way incense is used. A more thorough method is purification by steam. This is accomplished by heating up rocks in a fire, the same way sweat lodge rocks are heated. The rocks are then placed in a metal bucket, and water is poured on them. The steam that comes forth purifies whatever it touches.

Making tobacco offerings also became a daily practice. I would make tobacco ties before praying with the Canupa. These I gave to the Grandfathers in exchange for what I was asking of them. It was very important to maintain a balance between what I was asking and what or how much I was giving. The number of ties would vary from seven to 405, depending on the gravity of the situation. Occasionally I would also make prayer flags. These are an additional offering, mainly directed to the Grandfathers of the six directions.

Grandma had enlightened me about the four main Grandfathers, "posted" at each of the cardinal directions. These Grandfathers are also called the four winds, and many other names. They took their places at four distinct areas of the world, when the Earth was first formed. These main Grandfathers watch over the land and all its inhabitants. Each of the Grandfathers has special attributes, and they are identified by one of four colors: black, red, yellow, and white.

Black represents the west and the beginning. It is where the Thunder Beings come from. The totem animal was originally the Dog, but is now the Horse. Red represents the north. Its totem animal is the Buffalo. Yellow is the east, and its totem animal is the Black-Tailed Deer. To the south, the color is white, representing the completion of the circle. Its totem animal is the White Swan.

There is also the "above," to the heavens, represented by the color blue and the Spotted Eagle who watches over the world. The direction of downward, to the Earth, is represented by the color green and Earth's caretaker, the Mole.

I found it interesting that colors of the four directions are also the colors of the four races of humans. Through prayer, I noticed that each direction had a different "quality" that was specific to that direction. I could sense that there were many deep meanings to the concept of the four directions. I prayed for a more complete understanding, which I eventually did receive.

To the Great Mystery and to these main Grandfathers, I would pray as I loaded the Canupa with a special mixture of herbs. The mixture we smoke in the Canupa is red willow bark, osha root, and tobacco. The main ingredient is the dried cambium layer (inner bark) from the red willow tree.

Charles told us a creation story explaining why we smoke the red willow bark in the Canupa. "The Great Mystery formed human beings last, after all the rest of the world was made. The Great Mystery took pieces from each part of creation to make humans. According to this legend, some of the material from the cambium layer of the red willow was used to form the human lung. For this reason, it is smoked and used as a medicine for the lungs."

Much of this information was very basic, but at this stage of my experience, a strong foundation was being laid upon which future teachings could build. Deeper knowledge and understanding was only attainable after the first lessons were thoroughly learned.

Through prayerful dedication and a true desire to learn, I went deeper into my prayers. While using the Canupa to pray and communicate to the Great Mystery, I gradually found that the Canupa began to communicate back to me. I would suddenly have insight into the lessons that Grandma and Godfrey taught. Sometimes I would have mini-visions that answered my questions, or the information I was seeking would be revealed during the following day in some remarkable situation. The power of the Canupa opened up a doorway, and I found that information traveled through this doorway in both directions.

As I listened to the Canupa, I became acutely more aware of the responsibilities that human beings have. The whole experience of ceremony taught me that humans should always give before they take. We need to take responsibility for our thoughts, wants and desires. We need to be aware of the difference between what we mean to say, and what we are saying. We should walk on this Earth with prayer.

Each evening I would purify my room with cedar and sweet grass, often until the room was hazy with smoke. Then, by the light of a candle, I would load the Canupa. I would extinguish the candlelight and sit for hours in the darkness, searching for understanding.

I remembered the wisdom that Grandma shared with me. Grandma had explained that she prays for "health and happiness." She stated that all the prayers we say for good things could be broken down into those two categories. "Health always comes first, because without our health, there can be no happiness," she said. "Happiness is all those things in our life that we need and want. Needs always come before wants." Grandma also cautioned about asking for "wants" without considering the consequences thoroughly. She said, "We may desire something that we believe is in everyone's best interests, but not fully comprehend the repercussions."

Grandma also advised that the perceptions and vocabulary of the Grandfathers are not the same as that of human beings. The example she used was when someone prays for a "good" day.

Most people would understand praying for a good day to mean clear skies and sunshine. To the Grandfathers, a good day is often a rainy day that purifies the air and brings life giving water to all beings.

I also remembered Godfrey's many lessons. He instructed us on our responsibilities in the use of prayer with sacred tools, saying that people need to be very concise and focused. He explained that when it comes time for a person to speak their prayer in ceremony, they often start rambling. When one does this, the prayer loses its focus. He made clear that the Grandfathers are there to hear and help us, and they will give us what we ask for, but it's important that we be clear about what we want. He cautioned that if we don't have clear intention when praying in ceremony, and we start rambling, then our prayer becomes empty.

The other advice that Godfrey gave was, "People need to focus on the sponsor of the ceremonies." The ceremonies are for specific purposes, and that's what the prayers should focus on. People would often start praying for the trees, birds, the wind, and on and on. That isn't what the ceremony is directly about, and for the most part, the natural world is taken care of. "Nature isn't sick, it's people that have the problems, and we are causing trouble for the rest of world," Godfrey said. In ceremony, the one asking for the healing should keep completely focused on their desire for health. The other participants' job is to focus all their prayers on the one to be healed.

These lessons were essential, as they were the foundation to understanding this spiritual path. The most important lesson at this time was that spirituality is a way of life. It is a lifestyle that continually identifies and reinforces humans as part of a bigger world. The essence of this path is seeing creation as a family, and every component of the world as a relative. This is a way of life. Not like what I saw at church so many times, where people would pray on Sunday and then forget about their connection the other six days. What I saw with the Chipps family, and what I wanted for myself, was living prayer, living spirituality, and a strong connection to both the seen and unseen world.

CHAPTER 11 -BALANCE

Over the next months, I prayed with the Canupa almost daily. Sometimes it would be in the morning, but often I would end up praying at night. This I would do either in a room that was purified, or out in nature.

I would sit with the Canupa, sometimes for hours, with the stem pointed toward the sky. I would clutch the stone bowl of the Canupa near my heart, with my forehead resting against the stem. In this way I would connect my heart and mind as one. I had learned that prayers should be equal parts heart and mind. As Godfrey had instructed, in ceremony, the job of the Medicine Man, the drummers, the singers, the Helpers, and each person attending is to attain the state of "One Mind, One Heart," unified with the Grandfathers.

Being one in both heart and mind is often a difficult undertaking— even more so for anyone entrenched in modern society, and especially for a seventeen-year-old boy.

I found that often, there is a lot of energy in the form of emotion that radiates from the heart. This is a powerful force. I realized quickly that the emotions and desires of the heart don't always align with what is "best" for the rest of one's being. That's where the power of the mind should come into play. The power of the mind is to keep the heart in check and on track, and to make sure what the heart wants is in line with the rest of the being.

Looking back over my childhood, I saw that modern society didn't reinforce the idea of attaining balance between one's heart and mind. It often did the exact opposite, primarily by giving credence to one while negating the other — as if only one was operational at a time. I noticed that most people become either analytical and intellectual, or emotional and flighty. But when people think and act with both head and heart, a balance is achieved.

In the years that have passed, I have found that many people's physical sicknesses are manifestations of the imbalance between the heart and mind, expressed physically.

Besides praying with the Canupa, I also had opportunity to attend sweat lodge ceremonies at George's farm. The sweat lodge was left standing for this purpose. My family and some of the ceremony participants continued to pray and use the lodge with respect, in the best way we knew how at the time. We had been given this gift, but still didn't understand how to fully utilize it. We did the best we could, expecting that we would come to a better understanding over time.

I realized that the Lakota maintain a sacred relationship with the powers of the world; those that have existed from the beginning of creation. In order to access this power, many rituals and ceremonies have been developed. To contact the spirit world, and in particular the spiritual beings that the Lakota call Grandfathers, there are certain steps that are essential to each ceremony. Deviations from this "protocol" can make a ceremony weak or ineffective.

Godfrey and Grandma had shown us how to access the spirit world based on the ceremonies of the Chipps' lineage. I knew this was no small gift. My family and I honored what we had been taught by not deviating from the teachings, or corrupting the ceremonies with our own misconceptions. "Close enough" was never an option. The ceremonies had to be performed exactly as we had been shown.

Through the Chipps family, we were given the gifts of the Canupa and the sweat lodge, so we too could access the Grandfathers and form our own sacred relationship with them. Through the sweat lodge and the Canupa, we were entering a world no less real than the physical world we occupy. We found the spirit world has rules and laws that must be followed, just as the physical world does. The laws are different, but just as important. Deviating from these spiritual rules can be just as disastrous as driving down the wrong side of the road, or not watching where you're walking.

These sacred tools are a gift to humanity to benefit the world. They were given to human beings to help them walk a path of health and happiness, not only for themselves, but for all of creation. This is how I approached the Inipi and used the Canupa—not out of selfishness, but with a deep sense of responsibility toward the entire world

Through these ceremonies, we were entering the world of the unseen in ways that had previously been inaccessible to us. In that world, just as in the physical world, there are forces that are positive and others that are negative. By performing the ceremonies exactly as we were shown, and praying sincerely for health and happiness, we gained access to the positive forces of the spirit world, and we were protected from the negative ones.

I'm sure we made mistakes, but they were done from a place of innocence. We understood that mistakes would happen, but as long as we honored what we had been taught, there would be forgiveness. We also understood that if we intentionally deviated from the ceremonies or dishonored the traditions we were taught, it would unbalance the ceremony, and there could be dire consequences. If the ceremonies were not performed correctly, or if the participants allowed negativity into their prayers, then the protection from the negative spiritual forces would be weakened or completely absent. It was then that "bad things" could happen.

"Bad things happen if you make a mistake" was one of the first lessons Grandma taught me. This was one of the hardest concepts for me to understand. It has taken me years to come to terms with this. I think the difficulty I had in understanding was due to our modern lifestyle. We grow up and live in such a sheltered and protected world now that we have lost the full understanding of consequences.

It seemed to me that many people have a belief that anything a person does is okay, and everything will be forgiven, no matter what, without any sort of ramifications. In the traditions taught by the Chipps, there are repercussions if mistakes are made.

Over time I came to understand this "cause and effect" relationship, and how it is based on maintaining a balance. When a mistake is made, then something must offset that mistake.

To offset a mistake, one can either offer something, or make a pledge to complete an offering at a later time. I would usually make ties or prayer flags, and say prayers of forgiveness and gratitude. Later in my life, I would sometimes offer my life and flesh during ceremonies, such as pledging to Sundance.

There are different types of mistakes. There are mistakes of actions, thoughts, and prayers. Mistakes of action, as in placing a prayer flag in the wrong order, or stepping over tobacco ties, are usually done out of carelessness. These mistakes can be corrected by being more aware.

Mistakes of thoughts usually involve misplaced intention. An example of this is someone getting distracted by what they are seeing during a ceremony and not praying, or allowing their minds to wander.

A mistake of prayer is often because someone has negative feelings about some event in their life, and they are not able to set it aside, so their prayers are degraded and tainted by this negativity.

A simple mistake would be what Grandma called "One done out of innocence." This type of error involves an action that was not appropriate, but the offender didn't know any better.

An example of this occurred years after my first meeting with the Chipps family. I was living on the Pine Ridge Indian Reservation, working with Godfrey and the Grandfathers. During this time, I had a three-year-old son who found his way into the ceremony room while no one was looking. When his mom and I realized he was gone and where he went, we rushed into the room. We found him sitting cross-legged on the altar board, pretending to smoke a Canupa. Worried that this was a very bad offense, we went to Godfrey and told him what happened. He just laughed and said, "We'll teach him how to do it right when he grows up."

On the other hand, there are mistakes that are not innocent. The worst of these offenses is the intentional mistake. When someone knowingly does something wrong, the repercussions are ominous. Grandma spoke of an intentional mistake once, and it made me shudder when I first heard it. This event occurred during one of Horn Chipps' ceremonies. Horn Chipps, Woptura's son, was the originator of the Yuwipi ceremony as it is known today.

Once, when Horn Chipps was tied up for a Yuwipi ceremony and was standing before the altar, relying on his helpers to support him, they "dropped" him on his face. They did this intentionally, purposely trying to injure him. Why, I don't know. Grandma said when the lights came on after the ceremony, his nose was severely bleeding.

Within that same year, all three men died suddenly and tragically.

Grandma went on to say, "In a ceremony, the Medicine Man belongs to the Grandfathers. He is their tool. He is an instrument that they use to heal the sick and dying. A Medicine Man's life belongs to the Grandfathers, and they will protect him."

I also came to understand that it's the Medicine Man's job in ceremony to balance the energy. One component of balancing the energy is balancing mistakes. Because the medicine of the ceremonies and the life of the Medicine Man are intimately tied together, anything that unbalances the ceremony takes away from the medicine, and thereby shortens the Medicine Man's life.

CHAPTER 12 -NEW TEACHERS; NEW LESSONS

During the winter following the workshop and healing ceremony, Andy called to tell us that Godfrey and his family were coming back to Massachusetts soon. There were some people who needed the Grandfathers' help, and Godfrey was on his way. Andy had moved out of the Ashram and now lived in his own house. The gathering was to be held at Andy's new home, located 30 miles away in Becket, Massachusetts. We began to prepare at once for the pending ceremony, gathering wood and stones for the sweat lodges to come.

The room that was to be used for the ceremonies was a rough shell of plywood and had to be made ready as well. Luckily, my father was a carpenter. He and a few others set about making the room functional.

When the Chipps family arrived, there were a few new family members to meet. Godfrey's older brother Philip, along with his wife and young son, had also come to help with ceremony. One of Godfrey's teenage daughters had joined in the journey as well. Charles had remained in South Dakota this time.

Before they arrived, Andy told me that Godfrey's brother, Philip had been involved in a car accident a few years ago and was paralyzed from his waist down. He was now uncomfortably bound to a wheelchair

Philip turned out to be one of the most intense people I ever met. He had a presence about him that put everyone on edge. He was like an eagle that could see right through you. His eyes never missed anything, and he forcefully let you know if you were screwing up. He was the protector and guardian of the ceremonies.

Philip was Godfrey's older brother, friend, and defender. In the years to come, I saw him humble and frighten the hardest of men from the seat of his wheelchair. Just his stare was enough to make your hair stand on end. He had a warrior presence that conjured images of another age, when men road into battle with nothing but a bow, arrows, and the ferocity of a wolverine.

Grandma told me that when Philip was a young boy, Crazy Horse's spirit came into ceremony and gave Philip his medicine. She told me that Crazy Horse and the Chipps family were related in a way. "Way back in the 1880s, Woptura and Crazy Horse had been adopted brothers," she said. Grandma went on to explain that they had both been orphaned when they were young and adopted by the same woman. From this connection, they became both family and friends.

Crazy Horse and Woptura were lifelong companions as part of the same Tiyospaye (ti-yosh-pah-ye), or extended family group. Woptura helped make Crazy Horse a superb warrior by giving him medicine to protect him and his horse from injury on the battlefield. Crazy Horse became a fearless protector of his people. It's been recorded in historical accounts that Crazy Horse's very presence made people afraid.

According to Grandma, Crazy Horse felt a kinship with Philip and passed his medicine on to him. Maybe Crazy Horse did this to help protect the Chipps' medicine in this day and age. From what I saw with Philip, I believe it!

Once I got to know Philip, and he got to know me, he was very friendly. Philip was a gifted artist and the best Lakota singer I've ever heard. Even if there were ten other men singing in ceremony, Philip's voice soared above all. He also truly loved his culture and his people.

After Godfrey and his family arrived, people from all over New England, America, and the world showed up at Andy's. Many of these people had heard through the grapevine about the healing of the woman with multiple sclerosis and they wanted to see what this "Medicine Man" was all about.

Some people that came were in dismal need. Some had HIV or AIDS, and others had cancer. Their lives had been written off by the doctors. Many were told that they had only months to live. At any given time, there were ten to thirty people seeking help.

Godfrey usually stayed away from Andy's house until just before the night's ceremony. Occasionally during the day, I would see him pull in the driveway, speak to Andy and then leave. Once or twice he came to the sweat lodge to purify. During these times, he would talk to the people and share the wisdom of the Grandfathers.

It was then that Godfrey told us it was inappropriate to call him a "Medicine Man," and that he would correct people if they addressed him as such. The label for his job is a "Spiritual Interpreter." He explained that he interprets the voice of the Grandfathers. He is a tool that the Grandfathers use to help people. The Grandfathers heal, not him. He went on to explain that the term "Medicine Man" really only can be accurately applied to a handful of human beings. These are people who were born sacred—people like Woptura.

It was during these times of teaching that Godfrey, Grandma, and Andy would help newcomers to understand the lessons I had already learned. It was good to hear, and good to realize that in the past few months, I had already moved well beyond the basic foundation. Through my time spent with the Canupa, many of Godfrey's and Grandma's teachings had been clarified and expanded upon. As each lesson was understood, a new lesson was added; answers were often replaced by a new question. In this way, my understanding grew both in width and depth. I began to hear the words that Godfrey spoke with new ears, and understand the deeper meanings in the old lessons. These deeper layers of understanding only exposed themselves after I fully comprehended the previous level.

One of the most powerful new lessons that Godfrey brought to everyone was that of maintaining sacredness. The Grandfathers had spoken to Godfrey and had a very important message for us all. He stated this: "If we use a tool on sacredness, we profane sacredness. The only way to make this right is for the person using the tool to maintain the highest level of prayer."

Godfrey went on to explain that this is a critical issue that must be emphasized. He repeatedly said, "This is the most important thing for people to know!" He clarified the statement by giving examples of how it applies. He said, "Every time we cut tobacco-tie material with scissors, every time we carry a stone from the fire to the sweat lodge on a pitch fork, every time we cut down sage or choke cherry sticks with a knife, we are profaning what is sacred. We must pray as much as humanly possible to balance this profanity."

When I first heard these words, I didn't understand what the actual definition of "profane" was. After looking it up, I found out just how strong its meaning truly is. To profane sacredness is to abuse it, treat it with contempt or irreverence. I was immediately shocked to learn that even I might have profaned sacredness at times, something that went against my very soul.

This message instantly made me more conscious of my actions and conduct around ceremony—and in my life. Over time, I came to see that this lesson is one of the most important and life-changing teachings I've ever heard. From the Grandfathers' statement, I arrived at this understanding:

Each and every part of creation is sacred, as made by the Creator. Humans have been given the unique gift of being able to manipulate and alter that original creation, but our gift has a cost. The cost of our gift is that we profane the original creation every time we modify it with our tools. If we alter the original creation without the deepest prayer and respect possible, then we've degraded creation with our abuse. This leads to many unintended consequences.

To profane sacredness is to abuse our relationship to creation and our bond to the Creator. If we use a tool on creation, it separates us from creation. To balance this, humans have been given an even more powerful gift—and a responsibility—which has largely been forgotten today. This gift is the power of prayer and ceremony to balance creation. If we must use a tool on creation, we have to do it in the most prayerful way possible. We have to do it in a way that remembers that detachment and disconnection are not only possible, but likely. By praying, we can balance this act of disconnection. Prayer is communicating to the Creator and knowing the maker through the creation.

Looking around at the world today, I quickly came to see that the lack of understanding about how we are connected to creation—

and our lack of spiritual responsibility — are at the very heart of the most serious issues of the modern age. How often do we truly approach creation with this understanding? How would the world look if we all prayed whenever we used a tool on creation?

Would we still be strip-mining the Earth, or drilling for oil, or cutting down the forests, as we are now?

I eventually found the most effective way to maintain deep prayer when using a tool on sacredness was to communicate through prayer to the original creation and the Great Mystery, and then to alter the creation only as necessary, and only as the original creation permitted.

To this very day, I make whatever I do a work of art. Thus I am praying — while altering creation — in the most profound and reverent sense. By this, I mean that when I am utilizing tools, I create the most beautiful alteration of creation possible. I know that I am effective when I feel the same sensations I have while producing a great drawing or painting. I am altering creation, but balancing this profanity by praying, and maintaining my relationship with creation by working from the place of connection and creativity within myself — centered in my heart. In this way, I am able to sustain my reverent prayer while using tools on sacredness.

It was at this point that Godfrey and Grandma asked me to help people who were just beginning on this path. I was instructed to speak to the newcomers, helping them to understand the ceremonies and what was expected of them. From that point on, when a person came to the ceremonies looking for guidance and healing I would sit down with him or her and explain my understanding of these ways.

Because I was also tending the sweat lodge fire at the time, the beginner and I would sit at that night's fire and I would answer their questions, helping them understand what was involved in attending or sponsoring a ceremony. Using the power of nature and the sweat lodge fire as inspiration, I began to "translate" these ancient ways into modern English terms and bridge Lakota concepts into the modern age.

CHAPTER 13 - FIRE, STONE, WATER, AND BREATH

Over the following days and weeks, I continued to help with the fires for the sweat lodges and to educate new arrivals. Because of the cold winter weather, I often would be the only person at the fire. This gave me time to think and pray without being distracted. We were in the midst of a long, snowy, icy winter. During the frosty days and nights, I would wrap myself in a blanket and stay close to the fire for warmth. Sitting there surrounded by the freezing air and white snow, I would gaze at the yellow, orange and red dancing lights of the fire and asks for guidance. Looking into the flames, I remembered Godfrey saying that all knowledge comes from fire. During my time with fire, I came to understand its perfection.

Fire is part of a perfect circle. The light and warmth that the tree absorbed from the sun during all its long years of life is released in the form of visual flame and heat. The elements of the Earth that made the tree stand tall and strong return to the Earth in the form of ash. The gasses that the tree "breathed" are released back into the air. All this takes mere minutes or hours, even though it took the tree years to collect such energy. This energy is put into the stones and "brings the stones alive."

I also came to understand the stones better. In Lakota language, rocks are called "Inyan" (en-ya). They are also called the "Tunkan Oyate" (ton-gan o-yah-tay), the Grandfather Nation. In the Lakota worldview, all things that have physical substance are "alive." They don't consider a stone dead just because its life is different than a human's. Stones are considered the oldest form of life. They are the First Nation. In the Lakota creation stories, Inyan was the first being, and from Inyan came all other forms of life. Rocks are said to hold all the wisdom of the ages, even back to before the creation of the world.

I sat by the warmth of the fire, huddled in my blanket, watching the energy transfer from the wood into the stones. I watched this process and I could see the stones become infused with fire's energy. I knew the stones were fully charged when they glowed red. At that point, their true power is perceptible to the naked eye. It made sense to me that if "all knowledge comes from fire" and stones contain the wisdom of the ages, then when the two are combined, a person could have access to both wisdom and knowledge simultaneously.

I also realized the sweat lodge represents the universe. When the energized stones are taken from the fire and placed into the center of the sweat lodge, they represent the Earth at the beginning of creation. The sweat lodge is viewed as the "Womb of Mother Earth," a place of birth and re-birth.

In the Lakota tradition, one of the names for the sweat lodge is the Tunkan Ta Tiyoganake (ton-gan ta tee-yo-ga-nah-kay), or "the house of the young and the old." I understood this to mean we humans are the young beings, and the rocks are the old beings. The common Lakota word for sweat lodge is an Inipi (e-nee-pee), which means "life within."

After the "charged" stones are brought in to the lodge, the door is closed and the "Water Pourer," who presides over the ceremony after fulfilling the required training, pours water onto the glowing hot rocks. Water is the essence of life; water is the purity of life. When the purity of life comes into contact with the wisdom and knowledge stored in the hot stones, steam is formed. This steam is called the "Grandfathers' Breath."

As we sit in the sweat lodge and exchange our breath with the Grandfathers' breath, we absorb energy that increases our life force. The Grandfathers' breath changes us in profound ways.

Ever since my first sweat lodge, I have seen many people enter the lodge for the first time, and by the end of the ceremony they exit a different, changed person, with eyes a little more open. The power of the sweat lodge is purification and change.

More and more people began to come to Andy's house, seeking Godfrey. People had heard that there was a potent "Indian Medicine Man" who was willing to help "white" people. All the people that wanted to meet Godfrey would first purify in the sweat lodge. This was a requirement, and it introduced the new participant to this spiritual way of being. Many people came to Andy's seeking help without really understanding what the ceremonies were about. Their spirits had drawn them to this path, knowing subconsciously that there was a cure for their sicknesses. but their conscious, modern minds weren't necessarily ready for this leap of faith.

As these seekers of health and healing arrived, they would be guided to the sweat lodge. The sweat lodge would be their introduction to this spirituality, and also give them the opportunity to decide if they were willing to invest in this path; if it was congruent with their desire to live.

Before anyone entered the sweat lodge for the first time, they were educated on what they should expect inside the lodge. We always tried to mentally prepare the participants, explaining to them about the heat and steam.

One time a person wasn't educated before he entered the lodge, and this led to a comical situation.

On this day, it was late afternoon when a middle-aged man pulled up to Andy's house. He arrived just as I beat the ceremony drum to let the men know that the sweat lodge was ready. As soon as the boom of the drum echoed down to the house, all the men quickly walked to the lodge. The women remained behind and were busying themselves with final preparations for that night's ceremony. The man who had just pulled in began asking questions of the women at the house, but he was from Europe, and his English was broken and difficult to understand. He tried to explain that he wanted to meet Godfrey and wanted to know more about ceremony. The women, knowing that the men were about to enter the sweat lodge, rushed him up the snow-packed trail to where the men had gathered. They did not realize that he had never participated in a sweat lodge ceremony before.

He reached the lodge panting, his breath visible in the air. All the men, besides me, had already entered the lodge. It was a cold day, so they had quickly crawled into the lodge, and now anxiously anticipated the warmth of the stones. I was standing at the fire with pitchfork in hand, ready to start carrying the hot stones into the lodge. Between hurried breaths, this man began to randomly ask questions about Godfrey and the ceremony. I could hardly understand what he was saying.

With a confused look, he turned and poked his head into the doorway of the lodge, again asking unintelligible questions. Godfrey was not there that day. Andy was pouring water and was seated near the door, so when the man began asking questions into the lodge, Andy poked his head out and told him to just get undressed and hop in.

Not knowing what was about to happen, he listened to Andy and undressed. Quickly he crawled through the doorway, wrapped in a towel I loaned him. He ended up sitting directly across from the door, in the "hot seat." This is place farthest from the door. It is the area in the lodge that heats up the fastest and cools the slowest.

The rocks were blistering that day. Every one of them glowed brightly. The man didn't say a word. From my vantage point, I noticed his eyes getting bigger and bigger as stone after stone was brought in—35 in all. By the time the last of the stones entered the lodge, the men inside were sweating profusely.

As soon as the last stone was placed, I quickly undressed, wrapped myself in a towel and entered the lodge. The door was closed and Andy splashed dipper after dipper of water onto the sizzling stones. The steam burst up in wave after wave of searing heat. Suddenly, the man screamed in perfect English, "What the hell are you guys doing here!?!"

The door was speedily opened and the man scrambled out. After he cooled enough to talk, he explained that he just wanted to meet Godfrey and that he had no idea what a sweat lodge was. He almost decided this wasn't for him right then and there. Eventually, this unsuspecting visitor did get to meet Godfrey, and they became good friends. He was ultimately healed of his illness and is alive today. Godfrey always tells this story with a hearty laugh.

CHAPTER 14 - THE ALTAR AND THE WOPILA

Normally, Godfrey's older brother, Charles, set up the altar for Godfrey, but during this latest trip Charles had stayed back in South Dakota. I'm sure Philip would have done it, but his wheelchair made this impossible. So it fell back to Godfrey to take care of the altar while the Helpers arranged the rest of the Hocoka.

Grandma explained that it was very difficult for Godfrey to arrange the altar and maintain the energy balance for the ceremony. She told me that the ceremony technically begins as soon as people enter the sanctified room. Every person must be in constant and focused prayer from the moment they enter the room, until the moment they leave it. The Medicine Man's job is to balance the energy in the room. If any person in the room is distracted for whatever reason, Godfrey must use his own life force to keep the energy in balance. If the balance is not maintained, then the spirit world and the physical world won't merge properly.

Grandma then went on to explain that setting up the altar also calls for constant focus and prayer. Every movement, every thought, every second must be filled with prayer. "To focus on the altar and at the same time balance the energy in the room makes Godfrey's job twice as hard." Grandma recognized this and decided to do something to help her son.

Not long after Grandma and I had this conversation, she pulled me aside. It was about midnight, and we had just finished another ceremony. We were exiting the room when Grandma approached me with a big smile. She was very excited, and she wanted to talk to me right away.

Grandma quickly re-explained the issues with Godfrey setting up the altar. She told me that she saw the way I helped and how I approached the ceremonies. She said, "I know you truly believe in the Grandfathers." She went on to explain that during this night's ceremony, she had asked the Grandfathers if I could set up the altar. "They said yes!" she blurted out with a big grin.

Grandma went on with, "This is a great honor, and there are only a few people in the world that the Grandfathers allow to do this." I knew that for them to grant me permission to set up their altar spoke very highly of my faith and belief, but I could hardly believe it myself. This was not something that I had specifically asked for, and it caught me off guard. I did want to help with the ceremonies, but I didn't expect this. I was surprised and happy. Grandma was very excited.

That night, Godfrey asked for my parents to meet him back at his motel room. My parents dropped me off at our house before they went to the meeting. They were not gone long, and when they returned home, they were having a serious discussion. I was anxious to hear what Godfrey said. I repeatedly asked my father what he said, until finally he told me one thing. "Godfrey said you are ignorant."

I was taken aback...I asked for him to say it again. "Ignorant?" I asked. "What does that mean?"

My father just repeated the words "you're ignorant." I didn't really know how to take this. I knew to be ignorant meant I didn't know something, but it also seemed to have a negative connotation.

What didn't I know? I knew a lot... or so I thought, at the time. I wanted to speak to Godfrey. I wanted to get to the bottom of all this ignorance. With just one word, my excitement changed to confusion, and a little anger. Being told that you don't know something is a hard pill to swallow, especially when you're seventeen.

At the time, I thought I had the world figured out. Boy, was I wrong! Looking back, I totally understand what Godfrey meant. Knowing what I know now about the altar, ceremony, and life, I never would have rushed into it so quickly.

After that night, more ceremonies followed, night after night, one after another, and for the time being I continued to help with the purification fires. I hoped to talk to Godfrey about the situation with the altar, but he seemed to be avoiding me. Under Grandma's advice, I made a large amount of tobacco ties one day. I figured if the Medicine Man wouldn't talk to me, then I would just speak directly to the Grandfathers.

So, one morning I began to make ties. Each tie had a prayer or question in it. I continued to make ties until I had prayed and asked every question I could think of at the time. When I was done, there were well over five hundred ties. I wound the ties together into a large ball. I brought this bundle to ceremony and asked for it to be placed on the altar. That night, I spoke a quick prayer to the Great Spirit and the Grandfathers, asking for guidance and help in my life.

The Grandfathers heard me, and they had an answer. After the ceremony was over Philip slowly rolled his wheelchair close to me. He had a serious look in his eyes, but he spoke gently. He leaned over and told me in a soft voice the Grandfathers had an answer to my prayer. He said, "The heart is fascinated by many things, but if one stays on this path, then one will know the truth."

The words were so simple, and exactly what I needed to hear at that moment. I thanked Philip for telling me this. It was precisely what I needed to know. I had to be sure this was the right path for me. I didn't want to set up the altar just because Grandma or anyone else wanted me to.

Over the previous months, I occasionally had doubts that helping in ceremony was really what I needed to be doing, but now I knew. I instinctively understood that when the Grandfathers said "one will know the truth," they speak of a truth that goes far beyond just knowing the answer to my immediate concerns. I understood that if I stayed on this path, then I would know the "Truth" about everything. To me, understanding the Truth at its highest level was akin to understanding the mind of the Creator.

This message from the Grandfathers confirmed that I was going in the right direction. I knew now that if I held true to this spiritual way, I would eventually find what the Grandfathers had promised. This has put me on the path that I am still on today.

By now, we had been doing ceremonies for a month straight. Godfrey was spent. You could actually see him running out of energy. Over the course of the previous weeks, many people were healed, and many questions answered. I witnessed people being cured of many forms of sickness. People would finish their healing ceremonies and then go to their doctors to have check-ups. Many people returned reporting a full recovery. Even doctors called these "miracles."

It was during this time that I learned of the "Wopila" (wo-pee-lah). Wopila in Lakota means "I'm grateful." The Wopila ceremony is one of thanksgiving. It was explained to me that the Grandfathers generously help us during our times of need and sickness. This help is not to be taken lightly or for granted. The Wopila ceremony is a demonstration of our gratitude, and is the final piece of the healing process.

Grandma taught me that preparation for the Wopila ceremony is identical to the ceremony that one is giving thanks for. For example, if a person is sponsoring a Wopila for being healed during a Yuwipi ceremony, then that person will make 405 tobacco ties, prayer flags, food, and all the other items they previously made for their healing. The only difference is that instead of praying for healing, the person now says prayers of gratitude.

The Wopila isn't optional; it is a requirement of all who sponsor a ceremony. Unfortunately, for some reason the Wopila is often overlooked or forgotten about. I think it is a symptom of our modern society and our fast pace. We forget to be grateful. This can have calamitous costs.

During this month of ceremonies, a man came looking for healing. He had a heart condition and his prognosis was not looking good. He knew about natural medicine, and he knew that there were "alternative" treatments. He met Godfrey and sponsored a Yuwipi ceremony. Through the power of the Grandfathers, he was healed of his affliction. The Grandfathers also provided guidance to him on how to live a better, more balanced life.

His instructions were to make tobacco ties and offer prayers to Great Spirit and the Grandfathers every day. He was told that within the year, he needed to come back into ceremony and sponsor a Wopila. He was given a new life and was expected to walk his prayers in humility and balance, always being grateful. He said that he understood these instructions.

After a year, to the very day of his ceremony, he fell gravely ill. His wife rushed him to the hospital. He was having trouble with his heart again. He couldn't understand what was happening. He hadn't had any problems for a whole year. Why was he having heart trouble again? While sitting in the emergency room, he suddenly remembered his promise to sponsor a Wopila ceremony. It dawned on him that he forgot to formally say thank you! Right then and there, he said prayers for forgiveness and re-committed to sponsor the Wopila ceremony as soon as he could get to the Chipps family.

He was released from the hospital after a short stay, and he immediately went about completing his Thanksgiving ceremony. After this second brush, with death his heart sang with gratitude for the new life he had been given.

CHAPTER 15 -CONVERSATION WITH GODFREY

All too soon, the ceremonies were completed and the Chipps family was off to another location. I dreaded going back to the "real world." Again, I had missed a lot of school. Somehow I had to catch up, but I wasn't sure how I was going to do it. I really didn't have any trouble with class or homework; I just felt that school was a waste of time. Anyway, I was in a type of school, a spiritual school like no other in the world. I knew this was an opportunity that very few people ever get.

As it happened, I wasn't going to be able to make up what I had missed unless I attended summer school. No way! There had to be another option. After discussing my situation with my parents, it was decided that I would just attend college instead of completing my 12th grade year.

My parents supported me in my decision to drop out, get my General Equivalency Diploma (GED) and finish up the year in college. They understood how important this "Indian stuff," as they playfully called it, was to me. I think they knew that there was no way to stop me from doing it. I had put my mind and heart into learning and experiencing spirituality. This was my calling.

So I ended up withdrawing from high school and quickly attained a GED. Next, I enrolled in college. I attended a local community college and took many interesting courses. During this semester, I became a certified lifeguard. This was my introduction to modern emergency medicine. It was a year filled with good medicine.

Godfrey and his family continued to travel back to Massachusetts for ceremonies every few months. Usually, three or four different family members would come. They would do ceremonies for a few weeks, and then travel on to other locations.

One spring day, Godfrey showed up by himself. Godfrey's visit was not announced to the general public, and once he pulled in, only a handful of people even knew he had arrived. He seemed different— he was happy. During the past visits, Godfrey had been very reclusive, but this time he talked a lot and hung out with everyone. He suddenly seemed very human, and a very likable person, with a great sense of humor.

He would often tease his friend Andy, or joke about things that most people consider too "sacred" to laugh at. He seemed to have a smile just waiting to show itself, and his eyes twinkled with mischievousness. When the people gathered, he was always nearby or in the center of things; visiting, teaching, and joking. It turned out Godfrey had a sense of humor that I could really appreciate. It was nice to get to know the man behind the medicine.

The day after he arrived, we gathered at Andy's house for a sweat lodge and a "Five Stick" ceremony. This is an information-gathering ceremony. That day, I was tending to the fire. It was calm, cool and rainy spring day. There was a steady drizzle that saturated everything. Someone must have prayed for a "good day," I laughed to myself. The sky was gray, but the fire burned hot and bright. I was hunkered down and staying dry next to it. Suddenly, Godfrey was standing beside me. I had not heard him approach, and he knew I was startled. He stood there with a knowing grin from ear to ear. He asked me how the fire and the stones were. I quickly said everything was good.

Just before Godfrey appeared at the fire, I had been thinking about talking to him, but did not know how to approach him. I wanted to know more about what the Grandfathers told him in regard to me setting up the altar, and my place in the ceremonies. I knew that was why he had come to me by the fire that day.

Standing there in the misty rain, he began to tell me things. For the first time, but not the last, he began to talk to me about all I had been thinking, without ever asking me what was on my mind. He explained many mysterious and sacred things to me that day by the fire. He also gave me the opportunity to ask him questions about anything I wanted to know.

We talked about the power of the world and how people access this power. He explained the Lakota cosmology and the power of the Tunkan Oyate, the "Stone Nation." We discussed how every inch of the Earth is sacred and how this allows our prayers to move though the physical and spiritual worlds.

In our discussion about the Earth, Godfrey explained the Grandfathers had given humans a message. He said the Grandfathers warned us that we were at a critical juncture in the history of the world. The pollution being produced by modern life is making the environment unstable. The Grandfather advised that if all the machines in the world were shut off for seven years, the Earth would heal, and after that point the machines could be restarted. If that didn't occur, then the only way to heal the earth was spiritually.

This was part of the reason the ceremonies had been brought to non-natives, so we could all help right the wrong that was occurring to the Earth. I was shocked to hear Godfrey say these words because somehow I already knew this. Again, the words of the Grandfathers confirmed what I knew in my heart.

As we stood there next to the warmth of the fire, we spoke of a wide range of subjects, both spiritual and not. This was the first time we had a conversation like this. I got to know Godfrey much better, both as a man and as an Interpreter. He also got to know me. At this time, I felt there was true mutual respect between us.

Before long, the fire was ready and the rain had stopped. I announced to the men at the ceremony house that the sweat was ready by beating the drum. Godfrey beamed with anticipation. He looked at the white-hot, glowing stones with a broad smile and just said, "Good one, it's going to be hot!"

Godfrey poured the water that night. It was one of the rare times he joined the men in the sweat lodge. I could hear him telling jokes and making everyone laugh inside the lodge as I stood by the fire, ready to bring in the stones. He poked his head out the door and called, "Wana" (wah-nah), "Now."

I carried each stone with the pitchfork to the lodge with prayer. This sweat lodge ceremony felt different. There was an excited energy in the air, like something very special was going to happen at tonight's ceremony. It was a good feeling and everyone was happy.

After the sweat lodge was completed, every person gathered at the ceremony room. Godfrey was sitting in the room, visiting. This was not typical. Over the past year Godfrey would normally show up for a ceremony just as the preparations were complete and leave as soon as the door to the room was open.

Tonight there were only a handful of participants at ceremony, a core group of people that truly believed in the medicine. The people attending were Andy, my parents and I, and a few other people that had supported ceremonies for years. This group had a far different vibe compared to the days when forty completely oblivious participants would be tramping around. Their faith and level of experience was refreshing to be around. Godfrey had taught us well, and we now worked and prayed together with one mind; one heart. I believe this is why Godfrey was so relaxed and the ceremony was progressing so smoothly.

Godfrey announced that tonight, we were to have a special Five Stick ceremony.

CHAPTER 16 -FOUR LEVELS OF POWER

A Five Stick ceremony is used to get information. It is named after the five choke cherry sticks placed in the altar. This ceremony is subtle, but extremely powerful. Unlike the Yuwipi ceremony, there are no rattles, no whistles, and no dramatic displays from the Grandfathers. During this ceremony, a question is asked to the Grandfathers of the six directions, the sun and the moon, and all of creation. The Grandfathers analyze the question from every possible angle and direction, and then give a complete answer.

In many ways, this ceremony was more powerful than the Yuwipi, because all of creation is involved in the answer. To me, the Five Stick ceremony's power felt comparable to sitting by an ocean in the sunshine, feeling the winds of a distant but approaching hurricane. You feel the tremendous power that is approaching, and somewhere deep in your subconscious, you know it is impending by the touch of the gentle winds.

When all the preparations were complete, Godfrey pulled me aside. He said, "Tonight you are going to set up the altar."

"Tonight!" I exclaimed in shock. At the time, I thought I was unprepared to take this step. Looking back now, I should have expected this type of crash course. It's a standard method with indigenous teachings.

Godfrey always seemed to give a person a new task based on being spiritually ready, even if the person didn't think they were mentally ready. Needless to say, I was both very happy and honored, but also extremely worried. "What if I screw something up?" I asked.

He said he would be right there and would answer any questions that I might have. A quick explanation was given of the order in which each component of the altar was to be placed. It was mentally overwhelming. I was worried about making mistakes, but I wasn't going to back out... not now.

I understand why Godfrey had me set up the Five Stick altar first.

Godfrey's medicine has four levels to it. At the first level, the Medicine Man works with the Grandfathers of the Five Stick altar. This ceremony is about information, and the Medicine Man gains a tremendous amount of knowledge at this level. The Grandfathers continuously communicate to the Medicine Man, teaching and instructing him. Godfrey worked on this level from the age of thirteen to about eighteen.

The next level is the first "healing" level. It's at this level the Medicine Man first works with the Yuwipi altar. The Grandfathers of the Yuwipi altar are different than the Grandfathers of the Five Stick. These Grandfathers teach the Medicine Man about healing a person's spirit and body. Godfrey could cure most sicknesses on this level, but there were limitations. Certain diseases are rooted deeper in the spirit than others. Cancer is one of the most difficult afflictions of all to heal spiritually.

A major component of any healing is the openness of the sick person to be cured. The willingness to set aside his or her old life and truly live a new, healthier and happier existence is critical in any healing. The spirit must first be "wiped clean," and then the body can be healed.

The third level is also a healing level, but much more powerful. There is no disease that cannot be cured though this ceremony. Godfrey once compared the two healing levels as the difference between handing someone a scalpel in surgery, and being the surgeon that makes the cut. Healing ceremonies that would have taken days on the second level were completed in a matter of minutes on this new level. The ceremonies themselves also became shortened, like a powerful, supercharged version of the former level. With this increase of power also came an increase of responsibility, and an increase in backlash if mistakes occurred.

There is also a fourth level, which I never witnessed. From what I've been told, it's miraculous, even to people who grew up in these ways. I've heard that at the fourth level, the Medicine Man no longer needs a "ceremony" to cure people—just his prayers and presence heal.

At each level, the ceremony and altar is more complicated and powerful than the one before it. With the increase of power also comes the increase of consequences. By having me set up the Five Stick altar, I was starting at the appropriate level. I needed to learn, and learn fast. The Five Stick altar would teach me what I needed to know. Also, if I made mistakes, the repercussions wouldn't be as severe.

It was then I learned that by setting up the altar, I became responsible for not only my own mistakes, but any mistakes that occurred during the ceremony. Even though I was told this information before I set up this first altar, it took me years to fully understand what it means.

The altar is the doorway to the spirit world, and the person that builds this doorway takes on the responsibility for whatever happens next. When the spirit world and the physical world merge, then even the slightest mis-thought creates an imbalance in this new dimension.

The dimension that's created when the two worlds meet is like viewing a reflection of the world in a crystal-clear pool, but instead of just looking into the pool, we are surrounded by it on all sides. When a mistake occurs, it creates ripples in the water. These ripples distort the reflection and create an imbalance. The Medicine Man can smooth the ripples and bring back balance. This is accomplished with the energy of human life. Because I was the person creating the gateway to the spirit world, I also took on the consequences of offering my life when mistakes occurred. This was just one part of the "ignorance" I had that Godfrey once spoke of.

CHAPTER 17 -THE FIVE STICK CEREMONY

That night, as I sat down in the middle of the room, I said a prayer for help and guidance so my thoughts and actions would be correct. Up to that point in my life, I had never prayed so hard. All the components of the altar had been purified with steam and laid to my left side. My father was sitting on my right, burning cedar branches to provide continuous smudge. The only light in the room was the yellow glow of a nearby lantern. I took a deep breath and held it like I was about to jump into icy water. I reached out and picked up the first item, the altar board, and set down in its place.

Next I picked up an old coffee can filled with special soil that had been brought from South Dakota. I poured it out onto the center of the board. This soil had been gathered from a molehill out in the prairie this past summer. Grandma had once explained that moles push the dirt up from seven feet deep in the earth. She said that it's the purest soil there is.

I then picked up the prayer flags and passed them through the billowing cedar smoke. These prayer flags had been tied to choke cherry sticks that were painted black and red. I inserted the sticks into a row of holes on the far side of the altar board. They became the sentinel guardians, standing over the mound of earth at the center of the altar.

Next, I used my hand to pat the mound of poured earth into a round, flattened disk. The disk was then smoothed with a large tail feather from an eagle, removing any marks left by my hand.

After the earth had been smoothed, the tobacco ties were placed. Everyone that was attending the ceremony had made tobacco ties.

These I wrapped around the edge of the disk of earth. This was done very meticulously, so as not to make any marks on the earth. Once this was complete, I saw the ties are like the sky surrounding the Earth.

Sitting there before this altar, I became aware that I was witnessing the world take shape. It was like I was the Creator, shaping the earth, setting the directions in their place, and dividing the heavens and Earth into separate parts. I began to understand that the altar was a re-creation of the Earth, a miniature version of what the Great Spirit had made.

When the altar was complete, I came to see that the world I was helping to re-create wasn't just a miniature version of our physical planet. I was re-creating the reality of the people who sat in this ceremony tonight.

It was through this altar that the Grandfathers would hear our voices and answer our prayers. The answers would help each person make his or her world a better place...if they chose to listen. This in turn would ripple out to the rest of creation, making all of reality healthier. It was so simple, yet so profound. The prayerful combination of these sacred objects could literally change the world.

I continued the meticulous process. It took a very long time to complete this first altar, because I was so nervous about doing something wrong. I made continuous prayers for Godfrey's health and happiness. At this time, I understood that some of Godfrey's life would be diminished if I made any mistakes, so I constantly prayed for this not to happen. In my mind and heart, I begged the Great Spirit and the Grandfathers to take pity on us all.

The best way to describe my prayers for Godfrey, the altar, and all the people that participated in ceremony that night is simple. Love. This was the highest form of love, the kind of love that gives people the strength to perform miracles. The sensation of love radiated out from my heart and mind to all those who sat in the room with me, and through the altar, out to the entire world.

Finally, after well over an hour, the altar was set and now it was time to make the last offerings and load the Canupa. I spoke to Godfrey, telling him I was ready. He sat up straight and began to beat on the drum resting on his knee. He cleared his throat and started singing the Canupa loading song. Everyone joined in the chorus, and song filled the room. I felt a fantastic amount of energy pouring from the people seated around me. This force seemed to concentrate at the altar and myself. The hairs on the back of my neck stood up, and my heart pounded with the beat of the drum.

I drew a certain design in the earth at the center of the altar with a special sage root stick. Once the drawing was complete, I took pinches of the tobacco mixture and offered it to the Grandfathers, concentrating my prayer into the offering and focusing my complete intention on the Great Spirit and the Grandfathers of the six directions.

With the offering of tobacco pinched between my fingers, I extended my hand toward each direction one at a time. In a whispered prayer, I said, "Wakan Tanka, Tunkasila please take pity on us, come here and be with us. Hear our prayers for health and happiness. Help us to live." I then sprinkled each pinch onto the altar. Six pinches were offered in all.

Now it was time to load the Canupa. I took the wooden stem and the stone bowl, passed them through the cedar smoke, and connected the two parts. I then placed the complete Canupa onto a bed of sage.

The song that everyone was singing helped me remember the correct way to load the Canupa. Not the physical motions, but the mental focus that is needed. It goes like this:

Pipe Filling Song

Friend do it this way.

If you do it this way, your Grandfathers will see you.

You have an altar; remember this while making the altar.

If you do it this way, your Grandfathers will see you.

Friend do it this way.

If you do it this way, your Grandfathers will see you.

You have a Canupa, pray while loading the Canupa.

If you do it this way, what you want will be so.

Some people believe that this song repeats the same words used by the White Buffalo Calf Woman when she brought the original Canupa to the people.

It took me an extended amount of time to completely load the Canupa. Godfrey had instructed that there should be six pinches of the tobacco mixture placed in the bowl. Each pinch is offered to a different direction, starting with the west. He also advised that the sixth pinch should completely fill the bowl and be even with the rim. This was somewhat difficult, because it had to be exact, and I had never filled this particular Canupa before.

I took each pinch with a prayer. I desperately felt the tobacco mixture with my fingers and tried to only take 1/6th of the total needed to load the Canupa. I held out my hand while praying to each direction, one at a time. Starting with the west, I repeated the process until all six directions were included. When the last pinch was added, the bowl was luckily filled to its brim.

I smudged the Canupa one last time and placed it behind the altar. I quickly left the altar and took my seat next to Godfrey. The kerosene lamp was extinguished, and the songs of the Five Stick ceremony began.

The walls of the room faded away into darkness as the light was extinguished. We became immersed in the spirit world. Sitting there, singing in the darkness, the spirit world and the physical world fused into one.

I sensed a great expanse all around. Soon the power of the Grandfathers could be felt. I was in the presence of giant beings, whose feet were standing on the ground but whose heads were high in the atmosphere above. Their voices rolled across the sky like distant thunder.

Normally, a Five Stick ceremony lasts an hour or two at the most, but tonight we prayed and sang all night. The ceremony felt good, almost relaxing. Occasionally Godfrey would stop singing long enough to speak prayers and then a new group of songs would begin.

Even though there were only about eight people at the ceremony that night, at times it sounded like there were a hundred people singing. Our voices echoed across the room and the world. I heard songs that night that I have not heard since.

After many prayers and songs, Godfrey called out for light. From across the room, someone sparked a lighter into life. As the room was illuminated, it abruptly shrunk back down to normal size. The lamp was lit, and the Canupa was smoked. Godfrey seemed very happy.

After the meal was eaten and the dishes cleared, we all stood to leave the ceremony room. I was told by Godfrey to exit the room first. As I pulled away the black plastic and the blankets that covered the door, I could see light glimmering around the gaps in the door. I opened the door just as the sun rose above the horizon. Stepping out into the fresh morning air, the golden light twinkling through the tree tops caused me to squint. We had prayed through the night and were now coming out to witness the start of a new day. It was a good day to live.

Godfrey later told me that it was the first time since he became a Spiritual Interpreter at the age of 13 that he didn't lose any of his life from mistakes in ceremony. My prayers were strong, and they had been heard.

This was the beginning of an intense spiritual apprenticeship that continues even to this day. Godfrey has never ceased to awe me with his spiritual abilities.

CHAPTER 18 -TRAVEL TO THE RESERVATION, TIME WITH PHILIP

After my initial indoctrination to the altar, Godfrey left and went back to South Dakota. Before he left, he assigned my father and I a task. He made a recording of 38 ceremony songs. Out of these 38, we had to learn seven over the next month. These songs were specific to the Yuwipi ceremony.

For a month, I practiced the songs day and night. Wherever I went, I had headphones on and the tape deck turned up loud. Every chance I got, I would sit down with a drum and sing. Luckily, my room was up in the attic and my siblings were, for the most part, spared from my wailing. It was a difficult task, but by the end of the month my father and I could adequately sing all seven songs, though we had no idea what we were saying.

Godfrey returned to Massachusetts a short while later with Grandma and Philip. They had made this road trip to do a few more weeks of ceremonies. It was at this time that Godfrey decided only to do Five Stick ceremonies. All healings would have to be done back "home" in South Dakota. He explained that they had a sacred ceremony house on a very special piece of land, and that is where the people who came for healings needed to go.

I continued with the altar. It was nerve-wracking the first few times I set it up in front of Grandma and Philip...especially Philip. He watched me like a hawk. I could feel his stare, and I knew his critical eyes missed nothing. I think he was very skeptical that a "white man" could set up the altar to his standards. It took a while, but eventually he did accept what I was able to do, and how I was helping his brother.

Grandma was much more supportive and was always very proud of me. Ultimately, the only person I felt that could give me accurate feedback on how I was doing was Godfrey, and he seemed very happy with my work...so far.

I went to South Dakota the summer of my seventeenth year. Upon completion of this batch of ceremonies, my family and I were to caravan to the Chipps' ancestral land. I was elated to finally be making the journey to the origin of this power. I personally wanted to see the "source" of this medicine. I understood that the Grandfathers are connected to the land, and there is energy at the Chipps' residence that made the ceremonies stronger. I wanted to be immersed in this energy and find out more about its origin.

Within a few short weeks, it was time to leave for South Dakota. My parents still had about one week of preparation to complete before they could depart, but Godfrey and his family were ready to go, so I was leaving now. I would be riding in Philip's car as his relief driver. My oldest sister was riding with Godfrey, and Grandma. She was the relief driver in their vehicle. The plan was to drive non-stop to South Dakota, a two-day journey.

We left Massachusetts at sunset. The orange sun of late spring disappeared behind the western horizon just as we pulled on to interstate 90. I sent out a prayer for a safe journey.

Due to Philip's handicap he had a very unusual way of driving. He'd fashioned himself a stick with a T-handle at the end. He had sewn black leather around the handle to provide a better grip. Holding this stick in his right hand, he pressed the gas pedal or the brake, as necessary. His left hand controlled the steering wheel. At first it seemed a bit unsafe, but I found he was a very competent driver. I relaxed in my seat after a while.

Philip's approach to driving was reminiscent of the old nomadic horse warriors. His car was viewed as an extension of himself, like a war pony that carried him off to his next adventure or battle. He loved and respected these modern-day horses but also continuously pushed them to their limits. Sometimes he got "bucked off," or the horse would "break a leg" and have to be put down. There were many days over the past year that I observed him just hanging out with his war pony for hours.

Before this road trip, I never really got a chance to visit with Philip. To be honest, he intimidated me, so I avoided him. This road trip was the longest amount of time I spent with him, and through it we got to know each other much better.

I talked to Philip about my desire to help with ceremony and learn spirituality. He talked to me about the responsibilities of walking this path, and encouraged me to stay strong on it. "It's not an easy way to live," he said.

It wasn't until late in the second night that Philip began to tell me more about himself. I was driving, and Philip was sitting in the front passenger seat. For the longest time, the only sound I heard was the hum of the wheels on the road. We had just crossed the Mississippi and entered the eastern Minnesota prairie. The night sky opened up before us. A crescent moon hung low in the sky, and the Milky Way shone bright. The road was straight and flat. I knew this was the last leg of our trip, and I noticed the closer we got to South Dakota, the happier Philip became.

Looking out upon the landscape, Philip began recounting stories. At first it was as if he was speaking to himself, quietly, softly searching for the right words. Some of the stories were older than written history, while others had just occurred in the last few years. From the stories he told, I understood I was soon leaving "white" America. Philip's accounts were both exciting and tragic, often filled with violence. It was hard to understand how such powerful healing and such tragic events were both a part of the same history.

He told me stories of happiness, of times when the Lakota nation lived in balance upon the Earth. He talked about days long ago when the buffalo fed his people, and his people were a free nation. He told me about the power of the land, the stones, and the Thunder Beings. He spoke of the storms that roll across his beloved prairie, bringing destruction, but also new life.

 He then jumped to modern times and the current conditions on the reservation—the drugs, the alcohol abuse, and the violence. He spoke of gun battles between enemy families, the drunken brawls, and the chaos that alcohol caused. His stories reinforced that the old Lakota society had been virtually destroyed and replaced with a severely dysfunctional way of life.

Long before I met the Chipps, I had learned that the Lakota society was a warrior society. I remembered the old stories of battles and how glorious they seemed. Now, from what I heard from Philip, the fighting had never stopped. Unfortunately, the Lakota warriors no longer fought the cavalry or enemy tribes. They now fought and killed each other.

In Philip's voice, I could hear the anger and pain caused by colonization of his nation by "white foreign invaders." From what he was saying, I understood that this anger and pain has spread to many of his people. Philip spoke from his heart, and I could tell he truly loved his culture.

After hearing these modern stories of violence, the idea being a "warrior," which had always held certain appeal to me, began to fade. It seemed to me that being a physical warrior created a cycle of violence that could go on for a very long time.

Within Philip's story, there was also a thread of hope, peace, and prosperity. This thread was the Canupa and the ceremonies that his family preserved and now shared with the entire world. Philip, his brothers, and his ancestors were spiritual warriors.

I knew that I had also joined the ranks of the spiritual warriors. This is where I wanted to be. Spiritual battles are won through prayer, healing, and love. The challenges of being a spiritual warrior are just as daunting as anything the physical warrior faces, but through perseverance and faith, anything is possible. The wars I chose to fight are against the sickness and disease of the world. I promised to myself that I would do my best to bring true health, happiness, and understanding to the world.

On the early morning of our third day of driving, we exited interstate 90 at a place called Kadoka. Philip directed me to head south, just as the first light appeared in the east. In the early dawn light, everything still had a silver-gray look to it. From what I could see, the landscape was treeless, rolling hills covered with grass.

Just as the eastern light turned to red, the road dropped in to a lower basin, and these incredible rock spires ascended out of the prairie floor. The vegetation vanished and the landscape went from gentle rolling hills to a foreign land that looked better suited to another planet. We had just entered the Dakota Badlands.

The Badlands are like no other place on the planet. The fleshy earth is worn away, and the hard skeleton underneath it is exposed. It's a powerful and treacherous place. I felt that I was passing through some sort of boundary into another world.

We shortly passed through the Badlands and entered back into prairie. The sun broke the horizon, and I could see clearly how startlingly different the land was, compared to the eastern forest we had just come from. The geography now was rolling hills, creeks and washes. There were few trees. The ones I saw seemed only to line the low places. The hills were covered in grasses and sparse bushes.

It was mid-June, and the knee-high grass was still green. There was a gentle breeze this morning that made the grass sway and glisten in the newly risen sun. Small yellow sunflowers lined the roads and quick-winged birds darted in and out of bushes in front of the car.

We just entered onto the Pine Ridge Indian Reservation, home of the Oglala Sioux. This is the eighth largest reservation in the United States, with about 3,468 square miles of land and a population estimated at 28,787 residents.

The reservation was originally part of the "Great Sioux Reservation" established by the Fort Laramie Treaty of 1868, which encompassed approximately 60 million acres. In 1876, the U.S. government violated the treaty by opening up the Black Hills to homesteader and private interests. By 1889, the United States government had divided up the remaining land into seven separate reservations, leaving about 2.1 million acres over left to form the Pine Ridge Reservation.

This reservation became a prison for the nomadic Oglala Lakota. At first, they were not allowed off the reservation without specific permission from the Superintendent, a U.S. government representative who managed the reservation. The Superintendent worked for a new government agency called the Bureau of Indian Affairs (BIA). No longer could the Lakota wander the land as free people. They were encouraged to become farmers and ranchers, trading in their nomadic ways for a sedentary lifestyle. Ten communities were formed in various locations across the Pine Ridge Reservation. The town of Pine Ridge became the location of the central government.

The Pine Ridge Indian Reservation is famous for being the site of the Wounded Knee Massacre. On December 29, 1890, Chief Bigfoot and his followers were traveling to the town of Pine Ridge, seeking refuge with Chief Red Cloud after the murder of Sitting Bull. Chief Big Foot and his people were intercepted by the 7th Cavalry near Wounded Knee Creek, approximately 17 miles from their destination. A rifle shot was fired while the cavalry was confiscating all the guns in camp. The cavalry opened fire with their new repeating cannons and rifles, killing more than 150 people in less than one hour, mostly women and children. Many people believe this massacre was retribution for the Battle of Little Bighorn, where General Custer and the entire previous 7th Cavalry was wiped out.

The reservation and the site of Wounded Knee are also famous for the 1973 standoff between the America Indian Movement (AIM) activists and the FBI. The 71-day standoff made national headlines and highlighted the struggles of Native Americans for equal rights.

Currently, the reservation is composed of two of the poorest counties in the U.S., with unemployment on it hovering near 80%. The reservation population has the shortest life expectancies of any group in the Western hemisphere, at approximately 47 years for males and 52 years for females. Adolescent suicide is four times the national average, and the infant mortality rate is five times the United States national average.

As Philip and I traveled down the road, I had the sense that the unseen eyes of the ancestors and those yet to be born watched us pass by. The grandfathers and grandmothers of previous generations were looking to us to make life better for the grandchildren yet to come.

After exiting the Badlands, we came to a crossroad and took a right, now traveling on Highway 44. Soon we passed through a town called Wanblee (wam-blee). It is a small community on the eastern edge of the reservation. Wanblee means eagle in the Lakota language. The area where the town now stands was an old camping spot, back when the Lakota were still nomadic. The community was formed by people wanting to be as far as away as possible from the BIA-controlled town of Pine Ridge, located about 85 miles away. Wanblee grew in size and population after the Wounded Knee Massacre.

We continued past Wanblee and turned left onto a gravel road that led to what Philip called the "country." The country is the Chipps' family land, located seven miles outside of Wanblee. This land was given to Horn Chipps, back when the reservation was being divided up among the Lakota people. The "Chiefs" got to pick the location of their homestead.

On the way to the Chipps' property, I saw in the distance an enormous butte that rose a thousand feet above the prairie floor. Philip explained that the butte is called Eagle Nest Butte. It is approximately one mile long, and its width varies from 1,000 yards to just a few yards. There are wider areas covered with pine trees on the western and eastern sides. Philip said there was a path that runs the length from the east to the west side. Rising at the center of the butte, I could see the remnants of a steel frame that once was a lookout tower. Just past the eastern end of the butte stands a small, white, treeless butte. Philip said that was where the eagles nest.

From our angle, the butte looked to me like a Medicine Man in a Yuwipi ceremony, tied in a blanket and laid face down. I instinctively knew there must be some connection between this butte and Godfrey's ceremonies. It came to my mind's eye that this butte was someone's grave, maybe a giant of the ancient world that walked the earth long before people arrived. I wondered if this butte was the energetic center of the ceremonies and the reason we had to have healing ceremonies here.

CHAPTER 19 -THE "COUNTRY"

The washboard gravel road took an abrupt right turn. All the parcels of land along the rising and falling road were surrounded by barbed-wire fences. We sped down the road, past a couple of farm houses and a herd of cattle. After passing over a wooden one-lane bridge, we turned left through a gate in the barbed wire fence onto on a deeply rutted dirt driveway.

The Chipps' property spread out before me. Looking to my right, I noticed that it appeared that some of the land had once been tilled. I could still see the mounded rows in the earth. Philip said that his Grandpa Horn Chipps had cultivated the land years ago.

We drove about a quarter mile up the driveway to an inner section of land surrounded by a barbed wire fence. A dilapidated house and a decaying log cabin stood within this area. Even from the car, I could see both these structures were falling apart.

The foundation of the house was crumbling, and the roof sagged. There was no paint on the wood, and I noticed a bird poking its head out of a hole in the exterior wall. I was seriously concerned that the house would fall over any minute. The log cabin was even worse, with big gaps between its timbers.

Philip called the three-room, L-shaped house the "ceremony house." This is where Philip and his brothers grew up. He explained that Horn Chipps had built the house two generations ago. Currently, one of the rooms was occupied by Charles, one was used as a storage area, and the other room was kept empty and used for ceremonies. The house had originally been used by Horn Chipps for his ceremonies, and it is now being used by his "misun" (me-soon), younger brother, Godfrey.

Philip dropped me off next to the ceremony house. He currently lived in Wanblee and wanted to go home and rest, so he told me to wait there for Godfrey to arrive. I stood there, sleepy and disoriented, as Philip sped off down the driveway and back toward Wanblee.

I saw that there were a couple of vehicles parked near the house, but I didn't detect movement inside. I began to wander around this new environment, figuring out where I was.

The sun was rising fast and warming up the new day. Most of the morning dew had already evaporated off the grass. The ground was dry and dusty, like very fine sand. The air smelled like grass and wildflowers, and something else — whiffs of fresh manure.

That's when I noticed a herd of cows meandering on the land. I realized that the inner fence surrounding the house must be to prevent the cows from entering into this space. Outside the inner fence, there were many "cow patties" scattered across the land. Some were very fresh. I thought to myself, "I need to watch my step around here."

I continued to wander around the house. There was no running water on the property. The only water source was an old-fashioned hand pump, about 200 yards from the house. What I had originally mistaken for tool sheds turned out to be outhouses, strategically positioned at various locations across the land. All the outhouses were handmade and looked very weathered; one or two leaned precariously, as if battered by some recent storm. I poked my head in the door of one close to the house to find that it was a "two-seater." Weird! I couldn't imagine going to the bathroom while sitting next to someone. I mumbled to myself, "Maybe this is the woman's outhouse? They like to go to the bathroom together."

About twenty feet to the west of the ceremony house stood a log cabin. It was about 10 feet wide and 30 feet long. I later found out that this was Grandma and Grandpa's. They had built the cabin in the 1970s, and had preferred to live there while keeping the ceremony house empty. The log cabin also appeared to be on the verge of collapse. Its walls were bowed out, and its roof sagged. There were many spaces between the logs where the mortar had fallen out. A plywood door on the south side was unlocked, so I slowly opened it, hoping not to disturb anyone inside. No one was there. I found a pull-string light attached to an extension cord hanging from the ceiling. The light bulb illuminated a cozy dirt floor cabin. It appeared to me that the cabin was used as a cook shack. Along the inside walls were a stove, table, pots and pans, a refrigerator, and some shelves of food.

After leaving the log cabin, I continued to explore my new environment. The land was beautiful in its vastness, with rolling prairie in all directions for as far as I could see. The clear blue sky was enormous above me. Off to the eastern horizon, Eagle Nest Butte rose from the prairie floor. The property slanted toward a small creek that was lined with large cottonwood trees. Part of the creek had been dammed and held a fair amount of water.

Just to the south of the ceremony house was a plywood fence. On walking over to it, I found a large sweat lodge. The five foot high plywood wall provided privacy to participants as they entered and exited the lodge. The sweat lodge was impressive, but I was shocked to see the biggest fire pit in the world—at least eleven feet deep and ten feet wide. There were four steep steps leading down into the bottom of what could only be called a crater. The upper rim was composed of used stones from years of previous sweat lodges. As I walked around the base of the fire pit, I wondered, "How the hell is this going to work?" All I knew was that I would probably get burned.

Soon the summer sun became too intense, and I retreated to the shade of the log house, waiting for Godfrey to arrive.

CHAPTER 20 -SUMMER IN THE "COUNTRY"

Godfrey, Grandma, and my sister Sharma pulled in later that morning. It was about 10:30, but it felt much later to me after driving all night. The heat from the South Dakota sun had become extreme, so I was still hiding in the shade when they arrived. Godfrey got out of his car and stretched with a loud yawn. He then told me we were having a ceremony that night, and to start getting things ready. "No rest for the weary" became a common expression in those days.

It was mid-June, and the second annual Ellis Chipps Memorial Sundance was to occur next month. This Sundance had been started last year to honor the memory of Grandpa. At this time, Charles, Philip, Godfrey and Grandma were all making decisions on how to best conduct the dance, but Charles was stepping forward as the Sundance "Chief." Eventually, due to Godfrey's responsibilities with the Five Stick and Yuwipi ceremonies, Charles became the spiritual leader of the Sundance.

Wiwang Wacipi (we-wan-ga wa-chi-pee) literally means "dancing in the sun." The Sundance is a very old and powerful ceremony. For years, it was outlawed by the U.S. Government, and anyone caught participating in this or the other ceremonies went to jail. After the American Indian Movement of the 1970s, there was a great interest in bringing this ceremony back. Lakota elders and medicine people heard the call of the Oyate (o-yah-tay), the "Nation," and the Sundance returned, with some changes to fit the modern times.

People participate in the Sundance ceremony for various reasons. Some dance to give thanks to the unseen world as part of a Wopila. Others dance for healing, and still others for Visions. Because the ceremony contains components of other Lakota ceremonies, it can serve a variety of purposes. Even though each person dances for his or her own particular reasons, everyone comes together as a community to create the Sundance altar. There is much work and preparation that goes into the dance, and people from all over the world were arriving to help.

At the same time I stepped onto the country, many other people were converging on the property as well. Preparations for the Sundance were soon to begin. Some people had already set up camp and were getting ready to participate in Sundance, either as a Dancer or a "Supporter." Supporters are people who help in the preparation and the work of the dance, but do not actually take part in the ceremony. They are often aligned with a particular dancer.

By that afternoon, I found out that Godfrey and I had a full schedule. There were enough Five Stick and Yuwipi ceremonies to keep us busy for a month or more. I had met many of the people who were scheduled for the ceremonies back in Massachusetts, but there were also many new people. Most of the people that needed healing in Godfrey's ceremonies were not participating in Sundance that year.

I was also informed we would be having Hembleciya (ham-blay-che-ya), or Vision Quest ceremonies. The Lakota word Hembleciya translates to "crying for a dream." This refers to the "Quester" both physically and spiritually crying out to the Grandfathers for a vision or dream. A Vision Quest is an individual ceremony where a person goes out alone into the wilderness and prays for a predetermined of time. Sometimes this ceremony is called "going up on the hill," because people would often go up to Eagle Nest Butte for their Vision Quest.

The Vision Quest ceremony is frequently part of a person's healing process, and one of the "prescribed" treatments of the Grandfathers. A Quest is commonly done in a secluded area, like the top of a distant hill or mountain. At other times, it can be closer to where people live, but located in a pit dug deep into the ground. The person on the Vision Quest either chooses or is told the location for their Quest. They are also instructed on how many days and nights of prayer they will be doing. The altar of the Vision Quest is very much like that of the Yuwipi. There are prayer flags to the directions, 405 tobacco ties strung around the flags, and a bed of sage in the center for the person to sit or stand on. The Quester will stay in this area without food, water or sleep for one to four nights. While a person is on their quest, their Supporters pray over and maintain a continuously burning fire.

Upon completion, the Quester speaks of his or her experience to a Spiritual Interpreter, usually during a Sweat Lodge ceremony. The Spiritual Interpreter helps the Quester fully understand his or her experience.

I began to feel a bit overwhelmed with all the new information and tasks that needed to be completed. Up until this point, my introduction to the ceremonies and this sacred way of life had all been done mostly on my terms in Massachusetts. I had come from a place of comfort, but I now walked in a foreign environment.

The South Dakota prairie was much harsher then the gentle woodlands of the east coast. The natural energy of the land and sun was so intense that I felt at times like I couldn't handle it. Now that I was here, at the epicenter of this medicine, I felt inundated. On top of that, the introduction of the Vision Quest and Sundance ceremonies added another layer of intensity. I had a lot to learn, and there was much that I was expected to know.

Luckily, my older sister Sharma was there, so at least there was one person I could relate to, and we helped each other out. I think the whole experience was just as shocking to her.

CHAPTER 21 - INTENT

My parents, Gary and Judy, and my other siblings—Chelsea, Aaron, Davana, and Angi—arrived a few days later. My older brother, Darshan, didn't come on this trip to South Dakota. He remained in Massachusetts to work. While preparing a sweat lodge fire one afternoon, my family came rolling up the dusty driveway in my dad's '76 Chevy Suburban. Everyone was getting ready for another ceremony that night, so without unpacking, my parents immediately went to work.

The day after they arrived, we set up the tipi. I had been sleeping under a truck-topper placed on the ground as a makeshift shelter, so I was thankful for the improved accommodations. My father chose a campsite along a section of the creek, close to the dam. It was a beautiful area with lush green grass and huge cottonwood trees. I later painfully discovered that it was also covered in poison ivy.

This campsite was a great location, because it was far enough away from the hustle of the people around the Sundance grounds or ceremony house, but still within walking distance. The spot was a relaxing place surrounded by nature, where a person could slow down and re-center. As often as possible, I would sit outside the tipi in the mornings and watch the dragonflies shake off the morning dew before buzzing around. This time of relaxation would help me to get ready for the day.

The rest of the people staying out in the country were clustered in little groups, mainly near the Sundance grounds. We called these congregations of tents, "camps." There was the Texas camp, Thunder's camp, Morning Star's camp, and on and on. There was a lot of activity all over the Chipps' property, from sunup to sundown. Everyone had a job to do with all the preparations for that night's ceremony.

At the 2nd Annual Ellis Chipps Memorial Sundance, there were about 45 dancers and another 100 or so Supporters. There was a tremendous amount of work to be done in preparation for the Sundance: clearing a tract of property, the size of half a football field, of a year's worth of weeds; repairing or replacing sections of the pine "shade arbor"; gathering, sawing, and splitting over 10 cords of wood for the sweat lodge fires. Cooking and feeding the workers every day was also a massive undertaking. Everyone worked together at this time, and there was a real sense of community.

As the start date of the Sundance approached, more and more people arrived for Five Stick and Yuwipi ceremonies. There were daily car trips to the Rapid City Airport to pick up new arrivals flying in from around the world.

By the time "Tree Day" had arrived, marking the last day of preparation for the Sundance, we had already been doing healing ceremonies for over three weeks straight. Many people had been healed and many questions answered. Down at the Sundance grounds, people were anticipating the start of the dance the next day. It was a very special time, and everyone was excited.

Each night, the ceremony room was packed to capacity. There was room for 30 people to sit comfortably, but 40 or more people would show up. It was then that Godfrey began to have the Helpers and I restrict the number of participants.

He explained that many people attending the ceremonies were not there for the right reasons. The ceremony was exclusively for the sponsor, and everyone that attended had to pray for him or her with all their hearts. Anyone who entered the room and did not pray accordingly became a drain on the ceremony. It was critical to control this issue.

Personally, I would set up the altar and pray for the sponsor as if he or she were my parent, brother, or sister who needed the help. I would literally beg the Grandfathers for help and continuously pray for the sponsor to have a better life. Every person attending ceremony was expected to pray in this manner. Anyone that entered the ceremony that didn't pray, as Godfrey said, "with 110%!" is a drain on the energy available for healing.

Many people were turned away from ceremonies at this point, because they could potentially be distractions from the true purpose of the ceremony. Some people had hard feelings about this, but we knew that the ceremonies were not a show or that night's entertainment. Being a passive witness was not enough. I came to see that the healing ceremony is akin to an operating room, where every person present has a duty to provide the highest level of care for the patient.

At the same time, I also understood people's desire to attend the ceremonies and their frustration when we told them they couldn't. The energy that people feel in ceremonies is very intense. This energy can be addictive; it is like a natural high. The healing power of the Grandfathers is so potent that everyone who attends the ceremony absorbs a little of this energy. It often makes people feel happier and healthier than they ever have before.

The power of the ceremonies is to magnify our prayers and desires. It intensifies every action, word, and thought. This is what makes the ceremonies effective, and it is how the merging of the spirit world and the physical is possible. Because of this "intensification" we can, through prayer, bring the two worlds together in harmony and balance.

The medicine of the ceremonies increases the power behind our intent to the extent that, with the right focus, even a dead person could be brought back to life. But like all medicine, it is neutral. The medicine doesn't distinguish between a prayer for healing or a destructive desire. If a person's focus is on "bad" thoughts, then those will be just as intensified as the "good" thoughts. This can wreak havoc in people's lives.

Part of the lesson behind the good and bad young man in the White Buffalo Calf Woman story exemplifies this. Good thoughts will bring us health and life; bad will bring pain, suffering and ultimately death. When living this spiritual path and working with this medicine, one has to take total responsibility. Not only are we responsible for our physical actions, but we are also responsible for our thoughts, feelings, and desires. Spirituality on this level is a way of life, and much more than a two-hour stop at church each week. This is a hard lesson for many people of this day and age.

Over my years of experience with the medicine, I've seen many people healed by the power, but I also have seen many people learn difficult lessons. This is one of the basic understandings about the medicine that modern people have problems comprehending. Most people's introduction to medicine is through a ceremony, and they see the beauty and its power to bring goodness into their lives. What people have to realize is that within the medicine, there is also the power of destruction.

The main influence on the medicine, whether it is good or bad, is people. I compare certain aspects of spiritual "medicine" with modern pharmacy. For example, many of the pills people take have the power to help them in their lives, but if misused, that same pill can hurt or even kill. Spiritual "medicine" is the same in that it can benefit our lives, but it has to be used within the correct parameters, and in the right way. When using spiritual medicine, our intentions must be clearly for the benefit of all. Our actions must be conducted with prayer and love. This is the only way we can make sure that we are making good medicine.

This is just one of the reasons that we were forced to restrict who attended the ceremonies. Many people who were not raised in this spiritual way, or who had not had time to learn these basic concepts, did not fully realize the repercussions if they entered the ceremony with a distracted mind or any negativity. The lack of focus or negativity they brought with them would unbalance the ceremony, and the burden of maintaining the proper energy would fall to Godfrey, Grandma (who typically held the Canupa in ceremony), and myself.

There were times when everyone taking part in the ceremony was truly of one mind and one heart. That's when miracles happened. It's easy to see when someone is utilizing the medicine from a place of goodness. There was particular ceremony during my first summer in South Dakota that demonstrated this very well.

A young mother had brought her daughter of eight or nine years old to ceremony back in Massachusetts. Her daughter had cancer—leukemia, as I recall. Through a Five Stick ceremony, the mother was told to bring her daughter to South Dakota later that summer for four nights of healing.

The mother and daughter arrived a couple weeks after we pulled onto the reservation. They began to immediately prepare for a healing ceremony. This young girl sat in her tent all morning and made 405 tobacco ties, something that many adults were unable or unwilling to do. While making her tobacco offerings to the Grandfathers, she sang with an amazing voice. Through her song, she poured her heart into the tobacco ties. Her song and heart were so powerful that when people walked by, they would pause whatever they were doing, mesmerized. People would often stop and say a prayer for her before resuming their activities. This girl continued to sing all morning and into the afternoon. When she stopped singing, she had completed all 405 ties.

That night's ceremony was strong. As soon as the lamp was extinguished, the rattles danced and the eagle bone whistle sounded to the four directions. The floors and the walls shook, and the room was filled with joyous song and continuous prayer. The energy in the room sparked and crackled.

This reoccurred for three more nights and culminated on the last night, when the Grandfathers themselves handed this girl a Canupa, one that had been placed next to the altar to be blessed. It was the first time this had ever happened, according to Grandma. On that final night of ceremony, when the lamp was lit, this girl was sitting with Godfrey's blanket draped over her. In her hands she was holding the Canupa and Godfrey's medicine staff. The Grandfathers said that this child was cured and would live to be a very old woman. This was a very special young girl indeed!

During these four nights of healing, there was a Lakota elder who attended ceremony. He was one of the few elders left alive who had grown up in the "old ways." He only spoke Lakota, and he had only talked to Godfrey, Philip and Grandma the entire time.

That night, after the lights came on and the Canupa was smoked, he spoke to all that were present in broken English. He said passionately, "There is no difference between Indian and Whites in the eyes of the Grandfathers!" He softly repeated these words again and again, as if he had just come to that conclusion himself. He is right; we are all one.

CHAPTER 22 - RACISM

The Lakota are unique in that among many of the tribes of North America, they seem the most open and ready to share their religious culture with other people. The Lakota have a history of sharing their sacred information with whites from the very first contact with Europeans. Many books have been written on Lakota spirituality. It is said some non-natives have even gone so far as to become Medicine Men and Women, under the guidance of Lakota medicine people.

During this first trip to South Dakota, there was much talk about "white" people taking part in "Lakota" ceremonies. This was an extremely hot topic at the time, and everyone had strong opinions on the subject. The Chipps family had opened up the ceremonies to non-native people years before I had met them.

Grandma would often say, "The Canupa belongs to everything with a heartbeat. This includes all animals." Grandma and Godfrey explained that in the mid-1980s, the Grandfathers instructed Grandpa Ellis to take ceremonies off the reservation and bring them to all the people of the world. The Earth was in crisis. The world had become so unbalanced by all the pollution created by people, it could no longer be healed physically. Spiritual healing was needed.

People had become so removed from the natural world that we had forgotten our connection to the Earth. As people had moved further away from the Earth, new diseases "appeared," ones that current medicine could not cure. This affects the entire world and all its creatures.

Mother Earth was calling upon "medicine people" to step forward and help the human inhabitants to understand their place in the world again, no matter what culture they came from. Many spiritual people heard this call and began bringing what was once considered hidden ceremonies and knowledge out to the general public. These people who lived close to the Earth saw her suffering, and opened the ceremonies up to all people, regardless of race. Godfrey and the Chipps family were just one of many doing what was needed to heal the world.

Due to the spiritual call coming from the Earth, many "common" people were also pulled toward indigenous teaching. Suddenly there was an overwhelming interest in Native American philosophy all around the world. People looked to Native Americans for spiritual guidance and leadership. This continues even today. Perhaps even you may have heard this call within your heart.

Unfortunately, along with the genuine medicine people, there also came charlatans. Fake "Medicine Men" and "Medicine Women" began to pop out of every corner. Some of them had a little training, while others were pure hustlers. Some were white, and others were Native American, but had no true understanding of medicine. It was regrettable that these fakes lured unsuspecting people into lies, and they selfishly damaged people's outlook on Native spirituality and culture.

There were also many Native American people very upset that non-natives were being allowed to participate in "their" ceremonies. On one level, I could understand their frustration and anger. They viewed the ceremonies as one of the last possessions that white people hadn't stolen. Many of these natives view non-natives attending or sponsoring ceremonies as a threat, and the idea that a white person could become involved in ceremony to the level I was hadn't even crossed their minds.

But there was a deeper purpose in including whites in ceremony. If the world isn't healed, then all people, white and native, will suffer and die. This is not about who owns what. It is about the continuation of life on this Earth. As far as my part in the ceremony, I had to be the bridge between the altar and the non-natives. It was a heavy burden to take responsibility for all people, especially non-natives, who were searching for a spiritual healing.

From my experiences in the ceremonies, I learned that on a spiritual level, there is no such thing as racism. A person once asked Godfrey if the Grandfathers saw any difference between "Indians and Whites." Godfrey answered, "No, there is no difference." He explained that if you teach an Indian and a white person the same thing, in the same way, they will both understand it equally.

The differences between the races are a matter of perspective, more than anything else. A baby is born as a blank slate, and over the years he or she is taught to look at life from a certain point of view. This occurs on an individual level that reflects society at large. The perspective that a person or society has is only one way to look at life and the world. Ultimately, everyone and each society is dealing with the same world and same problems. What separates individuals and societies are our points of view.

The same issue is apparent with most religions. They are fundamentally the same but each has its own perspective.

It was during this first trip to South Dakota that I began to hear rumors about local native people having "issue" with white people in ceremonies. Some of these rumors, I later found out, were specifically about me. Word had gotten out that Godfrey had a white man setting up the Grandfathers' altar. I was fortunate that Godfrey protected and insulated me from those who were directing a tremendous amount of negativity toward me. Years later, I was told of a meeting between Godfrey and three native men who had come to confront him about white people's participation in ceremony.

One day, a person came out to the country to inform Godfrey there were three Native American activists in the town of Wanblee that wanted to talk to him about white people in ceremonies. They were not from Wanblee, but had traveled there to meet specifically with Godfrey. All three were old acquaintances of the Chipps family and had been part of the American Indian Movement. They had heard Godfrey was allowing a white person to set up his altar and tie him up. They had also heard that white people were participating in the Ellis Chipps Memorial Sundance. Apparently, this didn't sit well with them.

By now, I had been setting up the altar for Godfrey for about three months. I believe that Godfrey and the Grandfathers were satisfied, if not happy, with my work. I always did my best and prayed hard. I understood that what I was doing was not common among the

Lakota, and may have been the first time ever for a white person. I was oblivious to the rumors of racism, and I had no time to even contemplate it. I had my work to do, and that's all I focused on. From sunup to far into the night, I was busy with prayer and ceremony. I didn't even notice the day Godfrey left for the meeting. Later, this is what I was told took place.

Godfrey did not take this confrontation lightly. He was not happy about people questioning his or the Grandfathers' decisions when it came to ceremony. He walked into the meeting house and immediately took control of the situation. After reminding everyone present who he was, he asked what their concerns were.

At this point, they humbly replied that they were concerned that there were white people Sun Dancing, and a white man was setting up his altar. After a moment of consideration, Godfrey said forcefully, "Fine, we are having a ceremony tonight," and pointing to each of the individuals, one at a time he said, "You are setting up the altar!" "You are tying me up!" "You are singing the songs!" He left the house and returned to the country.

Needless to say, none of them showed up that night to help with ceremony. If they had, I'm sure Godfrey would have welcomed them with open arms and taught them all he knew.

At this time, because I needed protection and guidance in my work, Godfrey gave me a "Spirit Stone." Working in ceremony made me more susceptible to negative energies and people's negative thoughts. A Spirit Stone would provide protection from these destructive forces. This is a special stone that contains the spirit of a medicine person. It is a guardian spirit that has taken the form of a stone to help us in our lives.

A Spirit Stone is a direct connection to the spirit world and the medicine. It helps a person in many ways, not the least being to increase awareness. The stone acts like a microphone that transmits our thoughts and prayers directly to the heavens. It also "speaks" to us in a voice that we will hear. Each Spirit Stone is different, and each is meant only for the person to whom it's given. The stone also increases the intensity of our prayers and thoughts. People that carry a Spirit Stone must be mindful of their thoughts and not focus on negativity.

Often these stones are received in ceremony, after someone prays for help and guidance. Occasionally they can be found by a person outside of ceremony, usually in nature. A distinguishing feature is that you can often see a human-like face on the surface. I've seen Spirit Stones the size of pebbles, or as large as a football.

My Spirit Stone was specifically given me to protect and guide me in the ceremonies. Through it, I felt more connected to the source of the medicine. It guided my body and mind. If I was unsure about something, all I needed to do was ask, and almost instantly the answer would become clear. I knew my stone had a very special connection to the ceremonies, and it assisted me to be a better Helper. I wore it constantly around my neck, close to my heart.

I learned that I needed to care for the stone and treat it with respect. Spirit Stones must be cared for with frequent smudging. When entering the sweat lodge with a Spirit Stone, it is hung from the wooden frame above our heads. This is to give it a good steam, and also of out of respect. During the sweat lodge ceremony when the heat gets intense, we may lower our heads, sometimes all the way to the ground. We may not be able to handle the heat, but the Spirit Stone can, and it is wrong for us to lower them as we do ourselves.

The stone is part of the medicine, and needs to be protected just as any sacred item. Often people wear these stones as a necklace so it lies close to their heart. The stone is wrapped in sage, and then placed in a leather pouch. The purity of the sage protects the stone.

Spirit Stones will occasionally leave a person. This usually occurs because the person mishandled the stone. They might have let another person wear it, or exposed it to a woman on her moon time. One minute the stone will be there, and the next it is gone, and no amount of searching will find it. When this happens, a stone can be retrieved through ceremony, but a person must be careful so it does not leave them again.

CHAPTER 23 - A MONTH OF CEREMONIES

I was so busy preparing for each night's ceremony that I hardly even got over to the Sundance grounds. I saw maybe a total of ten minutes of it. A few short weeks ago, this would have bothered me, but now I understood that ceremonies are not "shows." I didn't want to go there just to be a bystander. I realized that someday I would be a part of this dance, but for now my hands were full.

I did take a few minutes to attend the big feast that occurred upon completion of the dance. The dancers were served lots of watermelon and all kinds of beverages to rehydrate them. With ecstatic looks on their faces, they seemed very happy and satisfied. I was amazed that most of the dancers weren't sunburned in the least, even after being in the sun for four days straight. A couple people just had rosy cheeks.

Before long, the camps were breaking and people were leaving to go back to their homes. The day after the dance ended, most of the people had left. The remaining stragglers were attempting to clean the area, but they seemed overwhelmed. I couldn't understand why all these people prayed for health and happiness, and then left the Sundance grounds in such a mess. It didn't seem right. At the time, I guessed everyone had to get home to the "real" world, and get back to work.

This was a pattern I observed with many attendees of ceremony. The western notion of "spirituality" where a couple hours a week of "attendance" at a church service, prepared and performed by others, was not how this spiritual path should be approached. Many people didn't understand that ceremony is part of an ongoing relationship; a consciousness that includes investing extensive time in preparation and closure. This includes honoring and thanking the site while restoring it to its original form. Spirituality is a way of life, not just a break from the "real world."

By the time the Sundance was over, we had been doing ceremonies for over a month continuously. From sun-up until well into the night, we lived, walked, and breathed prayer. Every night, there were one to four people sponsoring healing ceremonies. Often there would also be a few people sponsoring Five Sticks. There were always two sweat lodges a day—one for the men, and one for the woman. On top of that, there were numerous people doing Vision Quests who needed to be taken to Eagle Nest Butte at dusk, and brought back before the sun rose in the morning.

Eventually, all this work began to catch up with us. We were tired and the weather was hot. It was early August now, and the South Dakota summer heat was hovering around 105 degrees. Often the blanket that wrapped Godfrey during the Yuwipi ceremony would be so saturated with sweat, it would have to be hung out to dry.

Finally, Godfrey had enough. It was time to take a break. One day, he just disappeared. Before he left, he quickly spoke to my father, saying he was taking a drive to Rapid City.

This sudden change of pace was disorienting. I was tired, but my enthusiasm and desire to learn kept me continually motivated. I knew we all needed a break, but I still wanted to push myself to do more. My head whirled with all the new information I had learned, but I thirsted for more. I couldn't sit still either, not after being so active for the past weeks. Now that there wasn't a ceremony to prepare for, I felt totally out of sync. I wandered around the land aimlessly, feeling lost.

The next day, Godfrey showed up for a few minutes in a new red Beretta sports car. Over the past month he had been gifted quite a bit of money, and now he was spending it fast. He had just bought a new car and was renting a motel room in Rapid City. He stopped by the country on his way to pick up some of his family in Wanblee. They were going to "hang out" in Rapid City. I found out later that this meant they were going to party.

Over the past months, Godfrey had sacrificed his life for the good of all. For this, many people gave money and other gifts from their heart. He had money to spare and was enjoying the fruits of his labor. Unfortunately, part of the enjoyment included intoxication. It was the first time that I saw this side of Godfrey. I wasn't sure what to make of it. Up to this point, I had only known him as an incredibly powerful Medicine Man; I was now starting to see his more human side. I tried not to judge this aspect of Godfrey, and I respected his right as a human being to make these types of personal choices.

I eventually found out that even within the Chipps family and the Lakota community, people made distinctions when speaking of Benjamin Godfrey Chipps. "Godfrey" was the Medicine Man and Spiritual Interpreter. His very human side, people called "Ben."

At times it was like he was two different people, trapped inside the same body. Godfrey was the man who worked with the Grandfathers and translated their voices. Ben was the man who suffered from alcoholism and had as many, if not more, problems than everyone else. Alcohol was an affliction that not even the "holy" people could escape.

I decided that I wanted no part of this characteristic of Godfrey. If I was going to work with him, I had to make a clear distinction between Godfrey the Medicine Man and Ben, the common human. This distinction wasn't always black and white, but I did know one thing—I could not drink alcohol with him. My place, my destiny, was in ceremony, working with the medicine. I didn't want to have anything to do with the destructive forces that accompanied intoxicants. This was a very easy decision, because I met Godfrey to learn about spirituality, not to "hang out" with natives.

CHAPTER 24 -CULTURAL VIEWS

Before Godfrey left for Rapid City, on that day he handed my father a roll of money and told him to "Take a vacation!" So that's exactly what we did.

On that hot and dusty day, we loaded up my parents' '76 Suburban and headed to the closest metropolitan area, Rapid City. After working on the prairie for the past month, with the sweat lodge and a water hose our only means of washing up, we had become very grimy. We were all in need of a good shower with lots of soap. Also, during a recent adventure in the creek near the tipi, my younger brother and I ended up jumping in a patch of poison ivy. I developed a severe reaction that covered almost 25% of my body. I needed to soak for a LONG time.

We went to Rapid City, only slightly aware of the prejudice and racial attitudes prevalent in "white" South Dakota. My father is a full-blooded Italian, and the sun had turned his skin to a brown that rivaled any "Indian" on the rez. My mother, on the other hand, is mainly Irish. She is very fair-skinned, and the sun had bleached her hair to a whitish blonde.

Our introduction to the racial attitudes of Rapid City started the afternoon we arrived. We pulled into a local motel after a two-hour drive in the 100 degree heat without A.C. My mother went to the front desk and asked about getting a room. A short discussion ensued, and the attendant explained that they had a house for rent behind the motel, which she was willing to let us stay in for a few days. Ecstatic that there would actually be enough room for everyone, my mother quickly filled out the paperwork and paid.

The attendant then walked with my mother to the house, passing by our old rusty car with my dad sitting in the driver's seat. She gave him a dirty look, not realizing that was to whom she had just rented the house. After viewing it, my mother returned to the car with a smile. As soon as my mother walked to the old Suburban, the attendant put two and two together and panicked.

As we unloaded a few items into the house, there was a sharp rap on the door. Introducing himself as the owner, a gruff man hurriedly explained the attendant had made a mistake and we couldn't rent the house. My dad, being who he is, just said, "Too bad, it's already paid for," and closed the door in his face. Welcome to Rapid City!

The next four days were terrific. The Black Hills are a magical place of great beauty. After coming from the humid, wet weather of the east coast, the Great Plains had seemed dry and sparse, the Badlands even more so. It had been difficult to adjust to the lack of moisture while working on the reservation. But now, here in the Black Hills, there were beautiful, clear flowing streams, big trees, and wildlife everywhere. It was an island paradise surrounded by a harsh sea of grass.

We traveled around the Black Hills during the day, visiting the many tourist spots and hiking through the forest. One day, while hiking near the heart of the Black Hills, I watched as the moisture in the sky gathered together. Clouds formed and coalesced into a storm. What were once little puffs of water vapor soon became thick, dark clouds. Lightning began to crackle and split the air. Propelled by a gust of wind, the newly-born storm moved east out onto the prairie. Watching this storm move off, I was truly amazed. Now I knew why the Lakota believed the Thunder Beings reside in the Black Hills.

During our travels through the Black Hills, we ended up visiting Crazy Horse Mountain, strangely enough near a town called Custer. Visitors usually pay an entry fee, but it's free for Native Americans. The tollbooth operator took one look at our car and waved us through. Guess we still looked "Rez."

The mountain was, and still is, a work in progress. It looked like an old prominence made mostly of granite. At the top of this mountain, a blocky, unnatural face was visible. It was not refined, but one could clearly see the profile of a man taking shape. Below that lay a pile of stones that had been blasted off the mountain.

Carving this mountain to honor a person who died defending the ancient Lakota way of life seemed to me like a living contradiction. Crazy Horse was never photographed, so obviously the person that this mountain was being shaped into was someone else. I wondered how Crazy Horse would feel having a mountain in the sacred Black Hills destroyed in his name. I had the sense that he would not approve.

There was a museum at the base of the mountain that contained interesting facts and Native American crafts. While walking around the museum, I noticed pictures of the Chipps family. There were pictures of Woptura, the original Chipps, his sons Horn Chipps and Moves Camp, and one of Grandpa and Grandma. There were even pictures of some of the young grandkids I had recently met. Near the pictures, there were a couple of notes explaining that Chipps (Woptura) was Crazy Horse's Medicine Man and adopted brother.

I hadn't really realized until then what an influential force the Chipps family and this medicine had been on history. I remembered Godfrey explaining that both Crazy Horse and Woptura had been orphaned in their youth, and they adopted each other as brothers. But there was so much more I had yet to learn.

Godfrey explained that Woptura had been a true Medicine Man, and was born with powers. One of his powers was that of protection. Woptura gave this power to Crazy Horse in the form of a Spirit Stone.

This stone protected Crazy Horse in the battles waged against the invading soldiers and white settlers. Godfrey had explained that Woptura gave this protection to Crazy Horse, knowing full well that he was going to kill many people. He went on to explain that the "war" back in the 1800s was not about subduing the Lakota—it was about total genocide. During this time, the chiefs and leaders were being systematically murdered, and disease and starvation was being used to weaken the general population. The U.S. government encouraged Lakota dependence on the Fort system, which soon became "reservations." Crazy Horse was one of the few leaders who took a stand against the extermination of the Lakota way of life.

Woptura and Crazy Horse stood at the very crossroads of the Lakota Nation's clash with the western world. Woptura used the medicine to prevent his people from being wiped off the face of the Earth. He protected one of the Lakota's most potent war leaders, empowering him to deliver a devastating blow to the enemy.

Woptura and his sons also preserved the medicine and took it underground to save it from extinction. They preserved the medicine though the dark days, when even attending ceremony meant imprisonment. They ensured that the medicine survived and flourished by helping young Lakota men find their own visions and power. It is to their credit that the ceremonies are still with us today. Their dedication and sacrifice has preserved things like the Lakota Sweat Lodge, Vision Quest, Yuwipi, Five Stick, and even the Sundance.

Crazy Horse was one of the few leaders that stood against extermination of the Lakota way of life. Woptura gave him his medicine to prevent their nation from being destroyed. Now, after all this time, the medicine and the descendants of Woptura were helping the ancestors of the "invaders."

You could say it is twist of fate that the power of Woptura was now being applied to help heal the great-grandchildren of the very race bent on the destruction of his people. But then again, Woptura's destiny was to keep the medicine alive. In this he was successful. Now, with the help of Woptura's great-grandchildren, the medicine was spreading across the Americas and the world.

CHAPTER 25 -FORMS OF HEALING

We returned to the Chipps' property after a week in the hills. When we arrived, no one was around, and I guess my father thought it was time to be going back to Massachusetts. Quickly the vehicle was packed, and within a few hours we headed home. I didn't get a chance to talk to Godfrey, or anyone else for that matter. I was sad to be leaving, but really didn't have a choice in the matter, since I was still a minor. The journey home was uneventful and swift.

After arriving home, it felt like I had left a part of myself back in South Dakota. I tried to work and get back to the old routine, but I just couldn't manage. I continued to pray and make ties daily, but it felt like I was supposed to be back at the country. Months passed before Godfrey returned to Massachusetts.

It was early winter when he returned. Godfrey arrived one afternoon, and again he was the only one who came from South Dakota. Andy had lined up some ceremonies, and it was time to help once more. I finally felt "right" again, like this was what I was meant to do in my life. A weight had been lifted off my chest.

Helping with ceremony was never an easy job, but it always was the only work that ever made me feel complete. Even to this day, the only time I truly feel like I'm doing what I'm supposed to is when I'm in ceremony.

As new people showed up looking for help and healing, I had to educate them about spirituality. Many people initially wouldn't believe the stories they had heard of people being cured of AIDS, cancer, or other supposedly incurable diseases. They would say, "That's not possible," or "Not even doctors have a cure for that."

But when a person entered the ceremony, they would change their mind. Once they actually saw, heard, and felt the power, they realized that anything is possible. There is a certain awe and wonder people have when they first enter into the sacred space. The ceremonies show us what is truly possible in this life.

Through the power of the ceremony, people can find true health and happiness, but ultimately the result depends greatly on the person being healed.

Grandma often said that the hardest part of a human to heal is their spirit. The body's sickness is just a reflection of a sick spirit. It often takes years of unbalanced living for the body to become physically ill. Typically, the longer one is sick, the harder it is to be cured. Sometimes people would come to ceremony, and their bodies were so sick and wasted away that the best we could do was make their journey to the spirit world easy. During this latest round of ceremonies, a man such as this came seeking help.

With sunken cheeks and a long, straggly beard, he came one day, sitting in a wheelchair and surrounded by five or six people. He looked like a very old hippie. I couldn't help but think he had gone on way too many acid trips in his life. His eyes had a glazed-over appearance, like his mind had already partially passed out of the physical world. He said that his name was Morning Star, and apparently he was some sort of teacher. He had a following of mostly younger hippie types. He came looking for a healing for an incurable disease; what it was, I never knew. To me, he looked like he already had one foot in the grave, but that didn't stop us from praying for him. He sponsored a Five Stick ceremony that night.

After the ceremony, Godfrey told this man and his followers that the disease had spread throughout his entire body. He told them that we were going to be doing a healing ceremony, and that we would pray for him. Later that night, Godfrey let me know that the ceremony would only be to prepare this man for death. The best we could do was guarantee a smooth passing to the spirit world, and he would go where he needed to on the other side. I don't know if Godfrey ever told Morning Star this.

We did his ceremony and prayed for his soul. After that night, I never saw him again, but not long after the healing we were told that he died peacefully in his sleep, surrounded by family and friends.

This was the first time I saw a ceremony to help a dying person, and I realized what a gift it must be. It must have been this person's fate to find Godfrey and have his spirit wiped clean before death took him.

During a healing ceremony, the Grandfathers touch the sponsor of the healing. They usually do this by touching a person with the Wagmuha (wa-gah-moo-ha) rattle. Godfrey said when the rattle touches a person, there are 405 Grandfathers on the other side holding it. The term for this type of healing is Pajuju (pah-joo-joo), which means "wiped clean." This is similar to the Christian concept of absolving sins. When a person is wiped clean, all the past mistakes, transgressions, and unbalanced actions are removed. On a spiritual level, a person is given a new start and a chance to make a better life.

In a sense, the healing is like the death of the old life that the person lived. Through the healing process, people overcome and resolve their pasts. They attain true "closure" on their old life, and then in a magnificent, sacred moment during ceremony, they are given a new start. From this new start, they are given instructions on how to live and how to remain "healed."

In situations where a person is already passing over to the spirit world, the healing ensures spiritual help and guidance during the transition. The healing also wipes away the mistakes of the past and the person returns home to the unseen world as a pure spirit. This man, Morning Star, was very fortunate indeed.

The Yuwipi healing ceremony mainly deals with a person's spirit. Because this type of healing occurs on a spiritual level, a person must truly open him or herself up to the healing process. Some people, I found, are unable or unwilling to do this.

During this same session of ceremonies, a woman came looking for a healing. Like so many people before her, she had an incurable disease. This woman had lived with the disease for years. She explained that it was now progressing and taking a toll on her. She wanted to be cured and live a healthy life. I told her what she needed to do and how to make the offerings. On a physical level, she completed all her tasks readily and seemed happy, but when it came time for her to be "doctored" in ceremony, she was not healed. For some reason, she resisted the healing.

It was confusing to me at the time. Why would someone want a healing on one level, but want to be sick on another level? Shouldn't everyone want to be healthy and happy?

Over time, I have come to understand that there are different reasons for a person to hold on to his or her sickness. Some people, I believe, have chosen a path of sickness in life to learn or teach a lesson. Even though the disease is looked upon as an undesirable condition from a limited, narrow perspective, when looked upon by the greater consciousness of life, the condition reveals itself to be vital to the bigger picture. An example of this is the child that chooses to be born with an illness to help its parents understand true, unconditional love.

I also found that many people find comfort in their sickness. Their sickness provides them with the degree of attention they desire in their lives. This is often learned at a young age, like the child whose only means to get his or her parents' attention is to be "sick." People who grow up to understand that illness equals attention become adults who are very afraid to let go of their illness, even if it is killing them.

For others, the sickness is a mental illness which manifests physical symptoms. The mind has the power to produce any symptom in the body that it can imagine. Sometimes when a person has a deep mental illness, all sorts of outward physical symptoms will appear.

Another condition is that some people don't believe they are worthy of health and happiness in their life. This is also more of a mental problem than a physical one. If a person doesn't think they deserve to be healthy or happy, they won't be. It may take years, but eventually this belief will "attract" true sickness.

In situations like this, healing the physical body on a spiritual level is next to impossible. The first thing that must change is the way the people view themselves and their relationship to the world. Eventually, with enough desire, they may come to the point where they can accept the love of the Great Mystery. Only then can Grandfathers "wipe a person clean."

Before long, Godfrey went on to another location. He had work to do in other states, and then would be returning to South Dakota. I had just turned eighteen, and I was ready to leave my parents' home, but it wasn't time to leave Massachusetts yet. Winters in South Dakota are bitter, and it's next to impossible to have ceremonies then. Godfrey told me to wait, and he would send for me soon.

I ended up waiting until the spring.

Sal at 16   Sweatlodge and Tipi

Godfrey oversees Sweatlodge construction

Grandma Victoria Chipps

Eagle Nest Butte

Antoine getting the fire ready

Godfrey Chipps

Buffalo Nation

Ceremonial fire and Sweatlodge

Sundance tree Eagle Nest Butte

Sweatlodge altar - medicine wheel garden

The eagle's home

A stone medicine wheel

My sons and I

CHAPTER 26 -BACK TO THE REZ

Over the winter, I occupied myself with prayer and got a job at the local YMCA as a lifeguard. I felt like I was in limbo, not quite in one place or the other. My heart and mind were already in South Dakota, but my body just hadn't caught up yet.

It wasn't until early May that I finally left. Godfrey paid for bus tickets for my oldest sister, Sharma, and me. My sister had been holding Godfrey's Canupa for him during the healing ceremonies in Massachusetts. We were going to South Dakota to help with ceremonies and continue our education. I was excited, but also apprehensive.

This was the first time I would be leaving my parents, and I was only partially aware of how difficult it would be. I was very happy that my sister was going with me. She was four years older and had been living independently at various colleges for years. I knew she would know what to do and would help me, and I her.

My father was uneasy about us leaving, but in the end he took us to the bus station. I think he was worried that we were going to a dangerous place where he would not be able to protect us. I had confidence that we would be fine. I believed the Grandfathers would assist and guard us.

My father drove us to the bus station on a cool, clear morning. The trees were beginning to bud, but winter's chill still held its grip. Not much was said on the drive to the station. Hurried hugs and handshakes were our good-byes. We got on a bus in Springfield, Massachusetts, and headed west.

After three days on the bus, we arrived in South Dakota at a town called Philip. It's a small farming community located about 45 minutes north of the reservation. The bus pulled over to the side of the road, and we exited in the middle of nowhere.

We stumbled off the bus with sore legs from sitting so long. I felt grimy from three days without a shower. After our eyes adjusted to the bright morning sunshine, we saw that the only business nearby was a diminutive gas station. We meandered over to it and ended up standing by the side or the road. After waiting there for a few minutes, a big four-door car whipped up and came to a screeching halt. It was Godfrey's older brother, Charles. He rolled down the window, and with a Cheshire-cat's grin, told us to get in.

On the drive to the country, Charles was nice enough to buy us lunch. We didn't leave Massachusetts with much money and hadn't eaten a full meal for the past two and half days.

On the drive back to the country, I began to feel great happiness to finally be back in South Dakota. Spring was well on its way here. There was fresh green grass and new tender life sprouting up everywhere. The cottonwood trees had small leaves budding, and they shimmered in the constant breeze. The air still held a little crispness in the morning, but the day was warming. It felt good to be back, like coming home to a comfy house on a cold night.

My sister and I were greeted at Godfrey's new trailer house with big smiles and hugs. Godfrey directed us to a small travel trailer that we could sleep in. It had a bed that my sister could use; I would lie on the floor. I had brought a sleeping bag and a backpack with a couple changes of clothes — everything I needed.

Later that day, I went for a walk to the sweat lodge with Godfrey. He stopped near the doorway of the lodge. Standing there in the warmth of the afternoon sun, he pointed to all the stones that had been piled around the fire pit. The fire pit seemed like it had grown even bigger from when I last saw it the past summer. It was at least 10 feet across, and even deeper than before. The walls of the pit were eroded, and parts of it had collapsed to its bottom. The steps to the lower level, carved into the soft dirt, had become a steep, impassible slope. It looked like the winter snow and spring rains had been slowly reclaiming the pit back to the Earth. Now it was my time to make it functional again.

I could immediately see that there were many areas around the lodge that needed to be repaired before it was serviceable again.

The stones Godfrey pointed at had been used in sweat lodge ceremonies and accumulated over the past 10 years. These were rocks gathered from places like Eagle Nest Butte and the Badlands. They had been used in sweat lodges repeatedly, until they cracked and fell to pieces, and then were finally "retired."

Over the years, they had been placed around the pit. Mainly due to people's laziness, the stones had been piled in the front part of the fire pit, as it is the easiest to get to from the lodge's doorway. The rock piles in that area now stood four feet high, and almost reached the front of the sweat lodge.

Godfrey stood there in silence, as if in deep thought. I noticed over the years that he would at times suddenly stop talking, and this same blank expression would come over his face. I sensed that he was in silent communication with the spirits. Suddenly he snapped back to the moment and began to talk about the Tunkan Oyate, the Stone Nation.

He explained that when these stone are used during a sweat lodge, their energy is exchanged with the participants. A little of their energy goes to us, and some of our energy is absorbed by the stones. Not all of the energy absorbed by the stones is good, because some people enter the lodge with bad feelings. Pointing at the closest pile of rocks, he said, "When we get near this pile of stones, their energy can affect our energy. Possibly in a negative way."

Moving his arm through the air in a big, arcing circle, from the stones to me and back to the stones again, Godfrey explained, "This mass of stones needs to be like us, a balance of positive and negative." That meant the only way to stabilize the energy in this area was to evenly distribute the rocks around the fire pit. This would mix the negative ones with the greater amount of positive ones, thereby creating the balance. I knew this was my job. I was the one assigned to redistribute these stones around the pit.

As Godfrey turned and walked away, I felt a little overwhelmed and frustrated. Looking at the tons of rock before me, I mumbled to myself, "This will take all year!" Feelings of anger began to well up inside me. Why did I have to do this? I didn't make this mess... And then I took a deep breath.

After being around Godfrey over the past years, I knew there was more to his request than just moving stones around a pit. There were important lessons that Godfrey, and most likely the Grandfathers, wanted me to learn here. It seemed to me that everything Godfrey asked me to do had many layers to it. So I surrendered myself to the task at hand, knowing that I would understand the true purpose later.

I set to the job right away. I worked quickly and with prayer, picking up and moving each stone with the intention to align its energy. This was not only labor of the body, but also of the heart, mind, and soul. I worked at that stone pile for one week straight. I worked until my hands bled. I work until my palms and fingers blistered, and then turned into hard calluses. As I toiled, the stone pile was reshaped into a perfect semi-circle. I found that as the balance was made with the stones, I was also becoming more internally balanced. My intention to align the stones was actually aligning my own energy at the same time.

It dawned on me that this was the lesson I needed. Godfrey and the Grandfathers had me reshape the stone pile not just to balance the rocks around the pit, but create my own internal balance. The task I was assigned was not so much about stones; it was about my own positive and negative thoughts.

Once I had internal balance, I was ready for the next lesson.

CHAPTER 27 -ADJUSTING

After I had completed rearranging the stones around the sweat lodge fire pit, I felt more in balance and had more internal control than before. The task had been completed, and I was ready to move on to the next mission.

For the most part I felt good, and I was growing more spiritual every day. The only problem was, even though I had gained balance and control over my internal struggles, I was still weighted down. It felt like heaviness on my shoulders that I could not escape.

The weight I felt in part was due to all the recent changes in my life. The changes weren't just from moving to a new location and leaving my family home back in Massachusetts. I was also adjusting to a completely different society. I was vaguely prepared for this because of my previous trip to South Dakota and my years of helping with ceremony, but it was still a difficult transition.

During my first weeks on the reservation, I had to quickly let go of my old self-image. Even after years of helping and working with the Chipps family, I still pictured myself as young, independent, and savvy man — basically your typical American eighteen-year-old. I had grown up in "white" America and was accustomed to many comforts that were now gone. I had lived in a nice home, slept on a comfortable bed, watched T.V. when I wanted, and had all the food I could eat. I also had a loving family that provided me with emotional support. Before the move, I was also independent and could go where I wanted, when I wanted.

Now, here on the Pine Ridge Reservation, I was surrounded by prairie and dirt roads. The only water source was a hand-pumped well, or the rain that fell from the sky. There was no electricity, no radio, and no television. There were two-seater outhouses with doors falling off their hinges. Toilet paper usually was an old magazine or crumpled newspaper. There were no clocks or schedules. My entertainment was watching the clouds pass overhead or walking the acres of prairie. I was completely cut off from mainstream America. The closest I got to "civilization" was the occasional trip to Wanblee for a bath at Godfrey's ex-wife's house.

During this adjustment period, I was also being introduced to new aspects of the modern Lakota culture. I found that there are some major differences, and many minor differences, between the society on the reservation and white America.

Up to this point, I had not seen much alcohol and drug abuse in my life. Now it was everywhere. There were children younger than me talking about how adults drank alcohol because "that's what you're supposed to do." I would sit and listen as they would have long discussions about drugs and alcohol, full of great enthusiasm. For fun, the kids would suddenly break into a game of "AA." In this game, they sat in a circle and one at a time they would stand up and say their name, and that they were an alcoholic. Everyone would laugh so hard they'd fall off their chairs.

Many of the teenage girls had kids, were pregnant, or were trying to become pregnant.

This is the lifestyle they had witnessed all their lives, and now they were trying to be adults. All the teenage kids I met were trying to grow up and imitate their role models the best way they knew how. Most were aged far beyond their years. It's sad to look back now and see how these young, vibrant children were changed by a dysfunctional society.

Beyond the alcohol and drug abuse, I found the Lakota to be some of the most universally humorous people I ever met. Everyone loved laughing and teasing. The teasing was practically constant. Lakota joke about almost anything, including themselves. They see the humor in all things and everybody. After I realized that this teasing was basically all in fun, I really began to appreciate this ever-present sense of humor. I've seen many non-native people take great offense to this type of teasing. This is one of the smaller differences between Lakota and mainstream America, and it was easy to adjust to.

Slowly, I began to acclimate to this new culture in subtle ways that even I didn't recognize. On an intellectual level, I could identify the new information I learned and the knowledge I was gaining, but there were many more faint transformations that forever altered my perceptions of the world. Many of these changes I didn't consciously realize myself, until someone would point them out. My mannerisms, the language I used, and even my voice changed. People that did know me from before moving to South Dakota began mistaking me for a local.

It was during this time of transition from the "white" world to the "native" world that I received my first healing.

The healing that was scheduled that night was for a man with chronic pain. He had made his ties, food, and all his offerings. I had done my part and finished the preparations. Everyone was purified with cedar smoke and steam as they entered the room. Each person took their seats; women on one side, men on the other.

Godfrey was quickly tied and laid down before the altar. I took my seat between the man to be healed, and Philip, sitting in his wheelchair. The lamp was extinguished, and Philip began to sing the four direction song:

Yuwipi Four Direction Song

> *To the west a Grandfather Nation is coming to see you.*
>
> *To the north a Grandfather Nation is coming to see you.*
>
> *To the east a Grandfather Nation is coming to see you.*
>
> *To the south a Grandfather Nation is coming to see you.*
>
> *Above, Great Mystery*
>
> *Have pity on me.*
>
> *A nation is in distress.*
>
> *Grandfather*
>
> *Have pity on me.*
>
> *A family is in distress.*
>
> *Help me.*

As we sang these words, there was a sudden, loud rap at the door. It sounded like someone very strong was going to beat the door down from the outside. The pounding on the door stopped, and was replaced with heavy footsteps. We could hear someone or something walking around the room. It started at the door and began to walk down the space between the men and the 405 tobacco ties. The footsteps were so heavy, they could be heard over the singing. The hard wood floor sagged with every step, and it was getting closer and closer to where I was sitting. I would guess its weight was over a ton.

I was praying hard and becoming nervous. There wasn't much room between me and the 405 tobacco ties, so I pulled my knees to my chin and tucked my legs in close. I grabbed my legs and tried to pull my feet in even closer, giving what I now sensed was one heavy Grandfather as much room to pass as possible.

The footsteps stopped right in front of me. I then felt the softest touch on my toes. This Grandfather had stopped right in front of me, turned and stood with his toes gently placed on top of mine. I had never been directly touched by a spirit before, and I immediately felt an overwhelming sense of love.

Abruptly the rattles began striking my head and shoulders. It was startling and not painful, but very firm. The rattles repeatedly struck my head, shoulders, upper back and chest. Sparks of light sprayed out of the rattles and all over me. The sensation was overwhelming, and my emotions began to pour out. Tears ran down my cheeks.

The rattle then went to Philip. I could hear it thumping against his body, occasionally striking the wheelchair too. The rattle returned to me with a few more strikes, then back to Philip. Finally, the footsteps went slowly back toward the door. Again there was a loud crash at the door, as if it was slammed shut, then silence.

The song was over, and Godfrey's muffled voice from beneath the blanket called for prayers. Philip said a prayer in Lakota that I didn't understand, but I knew he was saying his thanks. I also said Wopila (I'm grateful) to the Grandfathers for the healing I had just received. The man that sponsored the healing only said that he wasn't touched. We continued the songs and prayers. Godfrey called for the "untying song" and was soon freed from the blanket. I could now hear him breathe clearly, and he spoke to everyone in Lakota, interpreting what the Grandfathers had said.

We ended the ceremony with a song that speaks about the tobacco tie and flag offerings.

Offering Song

> *Friend, I give you these, come and see them.*
>
> *On this day I give you these, see them.*

The lamp was re-ignited, and we smoked the Canupa. The meal was passed out to everyone present. I felt good, and the food tasted great. Godfrey sat in the corner of the room humming to himself, not saying anything.

On this night of ceremony, as always, we made a spirit plate. On it we placed a small amount of each of the food items that had been prepared. Back in Massachusetts, this plate would be set at the altar of the sweat lodge, or out in the woods, but now that we were in South Dakota the plate was taken to the family cemetery. This is located on a hilltop about one-half mile away from the ceremony house, on the highest point of the property. At the time, the only person buried there was Godfrey's father Ellis.

Over the past weeks, I'd usually taken the plate up to the grave myself. Most nights I would be able to find a ride from someone with a vehicle, and occasionally I would walk. Tonight, I had to walk.

Once the room was cleaned and all the people had left, I took the spirit plate and started to make my way into the night. I walked slowly to let my eyes adjust to the darkness. It was a moonless night, but the stars provided a faint glow. I had to be careful not to spill any of the liquid or food along the way. I began to silently pray and sing ceremony songs as I went. I always felt that bringing the food to the grave was a very special event, and I maintained a ceremonial state of mind.

As I was praying and walking toward the grave, I had a sudden change in my perceptions. I realized that the weight on my shoulders that I had felt for these past few weeks was gone. This heavy shadow that had been hanging over my head had suddenly dissolved away into the night. I was literally lighter on my feet. My step had its old happy bounce in it, and a smile broke across my face. The world seemed to lighten up, and abruptly the stars shined brighter. Even the Earth seemed to glow. I could actually see a radiance coming from everything around me, from all living things and the Earth itself. An invisible veil that had covered my eyes had lifted.

Joyously, I began to sing out louder and walk fast with renewed confidence. I felt whole again. I felt happy. This was my first healing.

A few days later, I spoke to Godfrey about my healing and what had happened that night in the ceremony. He said that a spirit that had promised to be his Kola (friend) years ago came into ceremony that night. Godfrey had called his Kola into the ceremony to help his brother Philip, who was having a hard time in his life. When I asked why the sponsor of the ceremony had not been touched, Godfrey explained that this man was not spiritually open to the healing. For a person to be healed, they have to be spiritually open and ready for the healing. Otherwise, nothing will take place. Godfrey went on to explain that because I was spiritually prepared, I received the healing instead. It was a simple explanation and made sense. I understood that I was ready for the healing because of my state of mind. This was in part due to the effects of rearranging the stones at the fire pit.

CHAPTER 28 -THUNDER BEINGS, HEYOKA AND PUPPY SOUP

After working on the stone pit and my healing, I was in balance and my heart was open. Through ceremony and Godfrey's teachings, I was learning something new every day. We had ceremonies for one reason or another almost continuously. Some days we would just do sweat lodge ceremonies. On other days, people would show up needing information or healing. Godfrey somehow always knew far in advance before anyone arrived for ceremony. He would start looking out the window of his trailer and watching the driveway, and would say, "Someone is coming for help today. Get the sweat lodge ready."

Occasionally, different types of ceremony would be conducted, or new components added, things I had not seen before. Not long after my sister and I had arrived at the Chipps property, there was a special healing ceremony scheduled. This healing was for a man with chronic back pain. He was not from the reservation, but had been living and learning traditional ways for many years. He had learned many aspects of the Heyoka "Thunder Beings," and on the day of his ceremony, he made an unusual offering that brought me to a deeper understanding of Lakota beliefs.

This man arrived early in the morning with a couple of young puppies. Initially I didn't understand what these animals were for. I thought that he may have brought them as gifts for some of the children. This was not so.

He took the puppies out of their box that afternoon and painted their bodies. He painted a red stripe down each of their backs, from nose to tail. He also painted blue dots, like hail stones, all over their fur. He took them to a pole, where a rope had been tied. Facing west, he wrapped the rope around one of the animal's necks, and in a quick jerking motion, broke it. The process was repeated with the remaining puppy.

After the puppies were dead, he singed the hair off their bodies using coals of a pre-made fire. Once this was completed, the innards were removed and the puppies were dismembered and placed in a boiling pot of water. I found out then that this soup would be part of that night's ceremony.

At the time, I didn't really understand this type of offering, or the fact that we would be eating it later. There seemed to be a deep spiritual meaning behind this man's actions that I could sense, but couldn't quite grasp. I knew there was a symbolic and spiritual message behind this sacrifice. I wanted to know more about what it all meant.

Unlike many people, I didn't have a problem with the fact that it was a dog. In my opinion, there was far greater respect in the way these puppies were killed then the animals that are killed for meat sold at the grocery store. I saw that this man took the lives of the puppies with reverence, and he had a strong purpose in doing so. I noticed the sacrifice of these puppies was directly connected to the Thunder Beings.

I had learned from Philip and Godfrey that the Thunder Beings were the spirits of the clouds and storms. They are one of the four sacred beings that contribute to life upon the Earth (along with the Sun, Moon, and Stone). The power of the Thunder Beings is change and purification. They bring about change and purification though rains, snows, winds, and tornadoes. Even the Bible talks about how they purified and changed the Earth during the Great Flood.

The Thunder Beings' power can bring about great destruction, but they also help sustain life upon the Earth. Their powers arise in the west, and the color black represents them. Certain animals are connected to the Thunder Beings. The dog, the horse, and the spider all have a very special connection to the Thunder Beings. A Heyoka is the Thunder Beings' human representative.

Heyoka are best described as sacred clowns. They are humans that the Thunder Beings have selected to demonstrate their power.

Heyoka do funny and weird things that make people laugh, but they also can be very frightening and mysterious. To be a Heyoka is to be a teacher of the dualities of life.

People know they have been chosen by the Thunder Beings through a dream. In this dream, they will see themselves from outside their bodies, like they are looking at their reflection in a mirror. They see themselves dressed in a certain way, or painted in a particular way. Even their hair may be different. Their bodies are often marked with symbols that specifically indicate the Thunder Beings' presence. The dream can be a very startling or unusual, and very lucid. Lightning and thunder are often part of the dream as well. It is a vision a person never forgets.

Traditionally, when a person has this dream, they go to a Medicine Man like Godfrey to have ceremony and find out what they must do.

Often, they have to do a Vision Quest first, and then they must go out in public as they saw themselves in the dream. Occasionally you'll see someone fulfilling their dream at a pow-wow, or some other social gathering. Their clothing and mannerisms are usually very funny. People laugh when they see a person dressed up like this out in public, but they also respect the power behind this display.

Heyoka have various medicines. One of the medicines they have protects them from heat. There are many old stories of Heyoka reaching into boiling pots of soup and not getting burned. They also have limited healing powers. One unusual thing about the way Heyoka heals is that if, for example, a person's right arm is hurt, a Heyoka will work on the left arm to heal the right side.

The offering of these two puppies was a very special event. After thinking about what I had been taught, I came to realize what a unique offering this was. I had been taught that each animal nation has a special healing power; its own particular medicine. The medicine of dog is very strong. As it's said, dogs are man's best friends.

Dogs and humans have traveled through life and upon the Earth for many ages together. Dogs were once the Lakota's only beast of burden, before the arrival of the horse. Dogs carried their burdens, helped protect the camp, and nourished the people in times of famine. The dog nation was once highly honored and respected. Dogs have an ability to love and forgive that is far greater than people. This is part of the dog nation's medicine. In Lakota belief, some of this medicine becomes a part of us when we eat this animal in a ceremonial way.

It is also understood that this type of food is not for daily sustenance, but is only eaten on very special occasions. When a dog is sacrificed in this manner, its spirit returns to the source of all spirit—the sky, what we would call heaven.

Through this sacrifice, I began to connect the dots between the knowledge I had been taught and the actual spiritual practices of the Lakota. Finally, I was gaining a more complete understanding of the Lakota cosmos. I was beginning to see how human beings interact with the world, both physically and spiritually, within this belief system.

Witnessing the sacrifice of these two puppies reinforced how vastly different the "white" world I came from was, compared to the Lakota world I was now living in. Though this sacred sacrifice, I experienced fully one more aspect of the duality of this life.

Heyoka Song:

> *To the earth I struck something, see it!*
>
> *To the earth I struck something, see it!*
>
> *To the earth I struck something, see it!*

CHAPTER 29 - PREPARTION FOR SUNDANCE

The transition to living on the reservation slowly became easier. Helping prepare ceremonies also became easier. I was adapting to my new environment, adjusting to this new life. I eventually found I was able to set aside my old ways of thinking and see the world from a new, healthier perspective. I was able to put aside my own personal weaknesses and unbalanced desires. I began to live in constant prayer.

A new world opened up before me. This world was one of a deep spiritual understanding and awareness. By setting up the altar, I had become responsible for more than I could understand, but the Grandfathers were helping me with this. My healing had wiped away much of my past, something that I was happy to let go. It had also given me a new life, a rebirth, which allowed me to grow in a new direction that otherwise seemed elusive. I felt a deeper connection with the spirit world. Through my intuition, I began to perceive knowledge that previously had been hidden from me. I also began to make better use of my mind's eye to help guide me.

Out of necessity, I also became more reclusive. I needed clarity of mind to fully deal with everything that was happening. My ability to feel what people were experiencing, and "see" the path they walked, was very intense. At times I was overwhelmed by all I knew about a person, just by shaking their hand. I can remember walking into an empty room, and all I could feel were the vibes left over by the people who occupied it. I'd have to leave the room and breathe fresh air to clear my head. I found avoidance of people the easiest way to deal with these increased sensory perceptions. On a spiritual level I was very connected, but on a "human" level, I became lonely.

At the age of eighteen, I didn't feel young anymore. I started to feel like an old man. I couldn't relate to most people my age very well. They seemed like kids, still having ignorant fun.

Time passed, and the month of July arrived. People started to pull in for the 3rd Annual Ellis Chipps Memorial Sundance. This year, I was to participate in the dance.

Just a few weeks before the dance began, Godfrey pulled me aside. He talked about the difference between learning from a teacher and finding the answers for oneself. He often would use the term "knowing something." I understood what he meant by this.

There is a big difference between having intellectual knowledge of something, and having a personal experience. At this time, I mentally understood many things. Some I had been taught, most I just instinctively knew.

What I was lacking was my own personal connection to the spirit world, the kind that Godfrey had. The only way a person can begin to have this connection is through a Vision. At this time, Godfrey and his ceremonies were my connection to the Grandfathers and the spirit world. I was using his Vision to fulfill my destiny.

Godfrey wanted me to find my own Vision. The only way to establish spiritual connection like his was through personal sacrifice and asceticism. This was accomplished through ceremonies such as the Sundance or Vision Quest. Godfrey told me that I would Sundance one day this year, and offer my own flesh for my prayers.

A person usually commits to Sundance a year before they actually dance. For most people, it takes a full year to mentally and spiritually prepare for this difficult undertaking. Over the course of the year the person walks in prayer, focusing on their reason for Sundancing. They make tobacco offerings daily and attend sweat lodge ceremonies as often as they are able. They pray with their Canupa, if they have one. The committed person walks a humble path during this year of preparation, and refrains from mind-altering substances or any other activity that distracts them from their prayers. During the year of preparation, a person truly walks their prayers, every day.

Over the course of the year, they also gather the personal items needed for the dance. This includes material and tobacco, sage, rope for a harness, bone or wood skewers, and the appropriate attire. Men wear "skirts" in the dance, and women wear dresses. Often, skirts and dresses are often highly decorated. Everything that is done is done in a prayerful manner, even picking the material for clothing.

My personal preparations for the Sundance began immediately. Because I previously had been living in a ceremonial and prayerful way, I was already mentally ready. What I needed to prepare were the personal items I would use in the dance. I quickly began to gather these items. Sage was picked and wrapped in red material to form a crown and bracelets. One of Godfrey's sons loaned me a skirt that he had used in a previous dance. Godfrey gave me an eagle bone whistle to use during the dance. I was given rope to form the harness that would hook me to the tree. I cut a choke cherry branch and shaped it into the pins that would skewer my chest. I had my personal Canupa wrapped in sage and tied with cloth. I made 405 ties and four prayer flags to hang on the sacred tree. I was ready.

The Sundance ceremony is a big event and takes a whole community of people working together to make it possible. Many people joined together this summer to dance and celebrate. Everyone chipped in and did their part. All the people who had gathered worked from sunup to sundown, getting ready for the dance. I knew the dance itself lasted for four days, but up to this point I didn't realize the entire ceremony went on for nine days.

But that didn't include the month before when, in trickles, people would show up and begin pitching in to prepare the larger grounds. This included mowing the half a football field sized patch of prairie, cutting wood for the arbor from a neighbor's property, and clearing creek beds of fallen trees to be used as firewood.

I learned that the first four days are spent in preparation for the dance, including purifying in daily sweat lodges. The dance grounds are made ready by people picking out thorn bushes and walking over the grass to pack it down. A pine bough arbor is constructed or repaired to provide shade to the supporters, as well as the singers and the dancers, during breaks in the ceremony. Wood is cut and stones are gathered for the sweat lodges.

The fifth day is called "Tree Day." On this day, a pre-selected cottonwood tree is cut down in a very special way. This tree stands at the center of the dance grounds, and is the focal point for the dancers' prayers. It represents the "Tree of Life," the force that unites and connects all life on this earth and in the universe. The tree is a ceremonial instrument of prayer and sacrifice.

On Tree Day, the dancers gather together and make prayers over the living tree. Before it is cut, the Medicine Man who is presiding over the ceremony prays and thanks the tree for sacrificing its life for the human nation. The tree trunk is marked with special red paint. A virgin girl then strikes the first cut on the tree with a new axe. After that the tree is cut down by the Sundancers, each taking a few swings with the axe. This is all done with continuous prayer and joyous song.

The entire community then gathers to carry the tree to the Sundance grounds. Once the tree is within the dance altar, it is placed on wooden supports, so it does not touch the ground. It is then secured and stabilized on the wooden supports, and the people are allowed to tie their tobacco ties, prayer flags and piercing ropes to it. After everyone completes attaching their items, the tree is hoisted up into place.

It is lifted into a pre-dug hole that is at least four feet deep. The whole camp helps lift the tree into a standing position. It is considered a very bad omen if the tree is to fall or touch the ground.

The process of cutting and setting the tree at the center of the dance altar takes an entire day, and sometimes well into the night. The morning after the Tree of Life is placed, the dance begins.

I didn't get to participate much in the preparation of the Sundance grounds this year. Godfrey needed me to help in his ceremony. We continued to do ceremony every night, right up to the day I danced. This year, I joined the dance at the very last day.

CHAPTER 30 - ENTERING THE SUNDANCE

The morning of my first Sundance, I awoke before sunrise. I shivered in the cool night air as I walked from the ceremony house down to the Sundance grounds, about one-quarter mile away. I could see that the fire tenders had been busy all night heating up fresh stones for the morning's sweat lodge. Silhouettes of the dancers began to appear, gathering together near the fire. The first glow of dawn illuminated the eastern horizon as the meadowlarks began to sing from their perches.

Approximately forty dancers had to purify in the sweat lodge this morning before entering the Sundance altar. The men sweated in one lodge, and the women in another. The men entered the sweat lodge without energy, most of us yawning as we said "Mitakuye Oyasin" while crawling through the doorway. It wasn't until the door was closed and hot steam hit our faces that we finally became fully alert. Life flowed back into us as we inhaled the Grandfathers' Breath deep into our lungs.

The warm steam felt good against my skin. I inhaled it, asking for the strength of the stones to be with me today. All the men prayed for a good dance and gave thanks for making it this far. Many of the twenty-five men in the lodge had been dancing for the past three days and looked exhausted. Beside myself, there was only one other fresh Sundancer in the crowd.

We exited the lodge, and steam rose from our bodies in the crisp dawn air. After I dried off, the next step was to load my Canupa. I sat before the sweat lodge and loaded it while someone sang the Canupa song.

The sun rose, and white rays of light shone across the prairie. The leaders called for all the dancers to take their places. We all dressed in our ceremonial garb. I had my red skirt tied tight around my waist. I wore a crown of sage on my head, and bracelets of sage around each wrist. My Spirit Stone pouch and an eagle bone whistle hung around my neck. Most of the men were clad in a similar fashion; our Canupas cradled in our arms near our hearts. The women wore full dresses made with many beautiful colors. The dresses were covered with silk ribbons that fluttered in the morning breeze.

All the dancers lined up in preparation to enter the altar. Men lined up in the front, and the women behind. I took my place at the end of the men, being that I was the last to join in the dance. From the front of the line, a shrill whistle sounded, and a chill ran up my spine. The singers began a slow song as we walked single file slowly around the outside of the altar, from the west side to the distant east gate. As we entered the east gate, we were smudged with cedar smoke. Each of us passed through the gate, raising our arms in the air and turning in a circle, honoring the four directions.

Once we had entered the dance grounds, the drum beat changed and the pace quickened. The leaders called out words of encouragement: Hoka Hey! The energy of the dance became palatable; it was both festive and reverent at the same time. Our feet moved to the beat of the drum, and we felt the pulse of the Earth.

The dancers were lined into rows facing toward the cardinal directions. First we danced facing west, then north, then east, and finally south. At each direction, we stood gazing off into the distant blue sky, sending prayers to the Great Mystery and the guardian spirits. After dancing like this for a time, we were eventually guided to a Canupa rack located within the dance grounds. Each of us set our pipes down in their places. We then walked to the Tree of Life at the center of the altar, touched it, and exited out of the west gate. Again we raised our arms and turned in a circle at the gate to honor the directions, and left the altar.

We were given a break. Most of the dancers sat or laid down under a shaded area built from pine boughs and ash posts. After no more than ten minutes, the leaders roused everyone to get back in line. Again we took our places in single file. An eagle bone whistle sounded, and the singers began a new song. This time we entered through the west gate. We were guided to dance in a large circle at the far edge of the altar. All the dancers stood in a circle; the women standing on one side, the men on the other, with the Tree of Life at the center. We danced like this for a long time. I focused my attention and prayer on the Tree of Life. Every step, every drumbeat, and every heartbeat became one unified prayer.

The leaders called and motioned for the all dancers to approach the tree. We danced toward the center. All the dancers came together at the Tree of Life, speaking our prayers or silently stating our reasons for dancing.

I was on one knee near the base of the tree. I reached out and put my left palm against its rough, woody bark. I prayed for understanding and knowledge. I prayed to have a strong spiritual connection and to truly "know something." I also asked to be the best Helper I could be, for the Grandfathers, Godfrey, and all the people that came to ceremonies.

The leaders called out for us to go take our spots back in the circle. We danced backwards and returned to our original locations. As I was dancing in the circle, staring at the tree and watching all the dancers moving to the beat of the drum, I realized something. I realized that we were imitating the Grandfathers and the Grandmothers in the spirit world. Standing on this altar, we were no longer just people dancing in the confined space of the Sundance grounds. I saw us as spirits dancing at the edge of the world.

My mind's eye opened, and I saw that we were colossal spirits with our heads in the sky and our feet upon the Earth, each of us standing at the edge of the Earth and praying for all of creation. In this moment, my eyesight became blurry, but my internal vision became clear. I saw many spirits dancing with us—not just the people with whom I had entered the altar. I had the overwhelming sense that we were all fulfilling our one true purpose. In this dance, we became the sacred Grandfathers and Grandmothers of this earth. We were the guardians and protectors of life.

This was the first time I had this vision and sense of reality. It was beautiful. I was so inundated by awe and sense of purpose that my eyes welled up with tears.

Sundance Song:

> *I pray to you on this sacred day with the pipe*
>
> *Grandfather pity me, my relatives and I want to be well*
>
> *I am sending a voice saying this*

CHAPTER 31 - THE PIERCING

Soon, another break arrived. We exited the altar and took our resting spots. The next round, I found out, was to be a "piercing" round. Some of the men re-entered the dance grounds and began to uncoil ropes attached to the tree. These ropes were staked to the ground in various locations. Their chests then were painted with a special red paint made from the dust of Pipe Stone. After a short while, all the dancers lined up and entered the altar. Again we formed a circle and danced. The men who had their chests painted were soon gathered together at the base of the Tree of Life.

One by one, they were laid down on a buffalo robe. Two incisions were made, about one-half inch apart, through the soft tissue of one side of their chests with a scalpel. The wood, antler or bone skewer each dancer carried was inserted through one incision underneath the flesh, and out through the other incision. In this way, the skewer was held in place by a strip of flesh. This was repeated on the other side of their chests. The men were then guided to the rope they had staked out prior to the start of this round. The rope was connected to either side of the protruding ends of the skewers to fashion a harness. Once the rope was securely fastened, the slack was released and the full weight of it pulled at the fresh wounds. Most of the men looked as if they were in ecstasy, while a few flinched in pain. Before long, the pierced men joined the dance, stepping to the beat of the drum. After a while, they danced back until their rope was taut. As they danced, the rope attached to their chest danced too.

The pierced men were then instructed to approach the tree. They danced forward, coiling the rope as they went. Once at the tree, the men knelt or stood, placing their hands on the tree. After about a minute, they were then instructed to return to their spots. They danced backward until their ropes were taut again. They approached the tree like this three more times, in the exact same manner. After touching the tree the fourth time, I heard a loud HOKA! (*Now!*) The men began to back away from the tree hastily, some almost running. Quickly, the flesh that held the skewers in place broke. Snap, snap, snap…their ropes shot back into the tree like rockets. Dancers blew on eagle bone whistles, and the women did a tremolo. Everyone cheered.

After the piercings broke, the men were led back to the tree one last time, and then guided back to their places in the circle. The piercing round came to an end, and we were led out for another break. There were still many men that needed to be pierced and offer their flesh before the end of the day. More ropes were staked out. The next piercing rounds were very much like the last one. This continued throughout the day.

It was nearing the end of the day before it was my turn. We were on a break, and the leaders said this was the last piercing round. The sun had long passed its zenith and now moved toward the western horizon. I knew my time had come.

With both anticipation and dread I smudged and entered the altar. I looked for a rope attached to the tree that was not being used and I strung it out. I pounded a wooden stake in the ground to hold the rope in place. A stone sufficed as a hammer. I then exited the dance grounds and was painted with the red paint. The Sundance leader dipped his finger into the paint and made two circles to indicate where I would be pierced. As the man looked at my scar-free chest, he joked with me about being a Sundance virgin. That was soon to change.

All too soon, the dancers were told to get ready and line up. I was worried that the pain would be too much for me. I was worried that I would falter. I knew what was coming next, and it frightened me, but deep inside I was confident that I would be fine. I took my spot and mentally checked myself. Yeah, I was ready.

If my prayers and wishes were granted, then all the pain and sacrifice would be justified. If this is what it took to deepen my spiritual connection and understanding, then so be it. With this confidence, I danced into the altar.

Once we took our places in the dance circle, the men with painted chests were guided to the tree. There were four men, including myself. The person guiding me did not touch me, but took hold of the sage bracelet that I wore. We walked to the west gate, spun in a circle to honor the directions, and then approached the tree. I was the last man to arrive at the sacred tree. All the other men were there, standing or kneeling at its base, praying out loud. One by one, the men were instructed to lie supine on a buffalo hide and were pierced. I was the last to go.

I was led to the buffalo rug, and a woman took my head in her lap. She stuck my sage crown between my teeth. I felt a sharp pinch on one side of my chest, then on the other. I thought, "Is that it? Not too bad." One of the leaders helped me to my feet. I felt lightheaded but ecstatic, and a smile broke across my face.

I stood and looked down at my chest. There were two chokecherry skewers held onto my chest by ribbons of skin and flesh. Blood trickled down to my abdomen. I felt no pain. A person then guided me back to where I had staked my rope. The rope was attached to my chest with a couple of loops; this was secured in place by the man that had guided me. Once the rope was firmly attached, the man said, "Hoka…dance!"

I began to move slowly at first. The weight of the rope pulled on my chest, causing short zings of pain. Soon I was dancing harder, the rope bouncing and dancing with me. Suddenly there was no more pain. All I felt now was a pulling sensation in my chest, and it felt good. I was attached to the Tree of Life, and I could feel its energy flow through me. The rope was like an umbilical cord, providing me sustenance. As I danced and prayed, the rest of the world melted away. Now it was just me the rope and the tree.

All the men who were pierced were instructed to approach the tree. I danced forward, coiling the rope as I went. Once at the tree, I knelt down, placing my hands on the trunk and prayed. I prayed for all of creation, for the ceremonies, for my family, for the Chipps family, for generations yet to be born on the Earth, for Godfrey, and for myself. I prayed that I would "know something."

We were directed to return to the ends of our ropes. I danced hard now, thinking of all the people that need these prayers. I knew that my flesh was a small sacrifice for such prayers. Again we danced to the tree, saying our prayers once more. This was repeated two more times. Finally after we had prayed at the tree four times, someone called out "HOKA!"

We backed away from the tree. I hit the end of my rope and it went taut, but I kept dancing backwards. I began to dance and pull on the rope, and suddenly, *snap*! The skewers tore through my flesh, and the rope shot back to the tree.

There was a great sense of release and accomplishment. A rush of energy flowed through me. I stopped dancing for a moment, feeling totally euphoric. I stood there, unsteady on my feet, wavering in the breeze, staring at the Tree of Life while tears ran down my cheeks — tears of joy and happiness. I had made a good sacrifice. I sacrificed the only thing that truly belonged to me in this life, a piece of my body. I spun around to honor the directions and went back to my place in the circle.

After we exited the dance grounds for our last break, a man called for all those who had just been pierced to go to him. One by one, he cut away the skin that remained around the piercing on our chests. These pieces of flesh were placed into red cloth, and then tied onto the Tree of Life. I had two oval areas on my chest where the skin and flesh had been ripped out. These wounds formed scars that would mark me for the rest of my life.

The final break was over, and we were called back to the dance grounds. The last part of the dance consisted of everyone saying their prayers of thanks and gratitude. All people from the camps gathered around the outside of the dance arena.

During this part of the ceremony, the dancers touch the people from the camps. They do this to help heal the people. It is believed that the dancers are sacred, and so infused with the energy of the spirit world that just touching a person could heal.

One by one, each of the dancers laid their hands on each and every one of the men, women, and children who had gathered. Some of the dancers touched the people with their Canupa, or a sage bundle they had been carrying. After the people were healed, one last pass was made around the Tree of Life. The dancers touched the tree and then exited back out the east gate. We danced all the way over to the sweat lodges. We continued to dance and raised our arms to the heavens in one last prayer. The songs ended, and the drumbeat rolled like thunder just as the sun sunk low on the western horizon.

This year's Sundance was complete. Now we had to take one last sweat, and wipe clean before we wholly re-entered the physical world. After the sweats were completed, the dancers and their supporters gathered in small groups to smoke their Canupas. They smoked and finished by saying Mitakuye Oyasin; "All my relations."

All the people then assembled to share in the final feast that had been prepared. There were many different types of drinks, and fruit of all kinds. There was fry bread and buffalo soup. It was all delicious.

CHAPTER 32 -PURITY

After the dance was completed, I spoke to Godfrey again. I felt like I'd accomplished what I set out to do during this Sundance. Godfrey explained that even though this year I had taken a step, it was still a small step. He explained that we have to keep dancing, keep sacrificing, and keep praying our entire lives. This was the only way to "know something." Even though I had received insight into the spirit world, I still had much to learn.

It was at about this time I started to date one of Godfrey's daughters. Her name was Julie and she was Godfrey's second-oldest child. I had met her in passing during the previous year. We had met at Grandma's log cabin, while she was making breakfast. This occurred the morning I woke up and realized that I had just spent the previous day jumping in poison ivy. The allergic reaction was starting to flare up, and I felt sick because so much of my body was covered in a rash.

On that hot summer morning, over a year ago, I stumbled out of the tipi before my other family members awoke and walked up to Grandma's log house. Julie was inside with her cousin and a couple of her younger sisters. I walked in and sat on a bench, not saying a word. I was groggy and feeling terrible, trying to resist scratching the rash. I silently watched Julie make pancakes and pass them out to everyone. She turned and asked me if I would like one, and I said yes. In that moment, I thought, "Someday she'll make a good wife for someone." The pancakes were delectable!

Now, over the past months Julie had spent a lot of time hanging out with my sister. She eventually began visiting us at the trailer where we stayed. I talked with her at night after ceremony, but during the day we didn't see each other much. Godfrey seemed unaware of our developing relationship, and Julie was hesitant to tell him. I thought it best not to say anything at the time either. I didn't think he would have approved. After all, I was his "altar boy," and he wanted to keep me pure.

The work I was doing in ceremony was good, and my prayers came from a place of purity. The Grandfathers say that until a person has had sexual intercourse, they are still pure. Godfrey knew that if I got into a relationship, that part of me would change. Purity is very important in Lakota ceremonies.

I was often reminded by Godfrey that the ceremonies were based on purity. Purity was the foundation of this spiritual way of life. One can trace this concept all the way back through the Lakota creation stories. Even in the White Buffalo Calf Woman story, the underlying theme is one of purity. The Lakota creation legends reinforce the importance of this. Godfrey's ceremonies came from the same source, so purity was essential.

These techniques and practices were to ensure or enhance purity. The sweat lodge, the steaming, and the smudging were all to ensure physical, mental, and spiritual purity. People maintained themselves in a state of purity through constant prayer. All this was to make the ceremony's foundation strong. At this time I was still a virgin, so I also had more innate purity. Godfrey knew this, and so did I. But I also knew that I could not remain a virgin the rest of my life. A change occurred in my life during this summer.

One night, my sister did not stay in the trailer. She spent the night in Wanblee at Godfrey's ex-wife's house. That night, after I completed the ceremony and brought the spirit plate to the grave, I met Julie back at the trailer. A wind had kicked up; there was a thunderstorm approaching in the distance. As I walked into the trailer, the wind slammed the door shut behind me. Julie was lying in the bed.

Somewhere in the back of my mind, I was scared of the changes that would occur, but I couldn't turn back now. I asked Julie if she was ready for all of this and everything it meant, and she said yes. I knew if we did this, that we would be bound together as a married couple, I wanted to make sure she understood this.

The thunderstorm came and shook the trailer. Lightning flashed across the sky, and in the distance the horses whinnied. I knew change had come, and a bridge had been crossed that could never be crossed again. This was the beginning of a relationship that brought both great happiness and great sorrow into my life.

Not too long after this, my parents and younger siblings moved from Massachusetts to South Dakota. They ended up living at the Chipps' "Country," as it was called, in their tipi for most of the summer and into late fall. Eventually my dad bought a single-wide trailer that was moved up near the ceremony house. My sister moved out of our little trailer and stayed with my parents to give Julie and I more time together.

My parents continued to help and support ceremonies. My younger siblings also helped out at times, but they were still young kids and were enjoying life.

After Julie and I became a couple, I continued to help with ceremonies as if nothing had changed. I didn't feel different, but I still worried that the effectiveness of my prayer was diminished. Godfrey didn't say anything to me, but he eventually found out about Julie and me. One of his younger daughters told him. Godfrey only said it was good for Julie, because I was a hard worker and she would have everything she wants.

I didn't notice any major changes in ceremony right away, but over time I did notice subtle differences in myself. Internally, I felt less connected to the spirit and more connected to the flesh. I had anticipated this change. In my mind, it was a fair trade for my relationship. I knew eventually a child would be born who would carry the purity I once had.

Julie already had a child from a previous relationship. His name was Antoine, and he was about two years old when Julie and I first dated. For the most part, he had not been at the Country during our initial time together. When Julie stayed in the Country, Antoine would usually reside with his grandmother in Wanblee. Eventually, Antoine began to stay at the trailer with us. He was a good kid, always full of questions. He talked so much that my sister called him Antoine La Bouché, or just La Bouché, or "The Mouth." Antoine liked to play with toy cars in the dirt and was usually caked with mud and dust from head to toe. I tried to be a good role model and teach him what I knew.

Summer wore away to fall. Sundance had come and passed. During the summer months, the land was full of people coming and going. Now that everyone had gone, it seemed lonely and desolate. Eventually snow began to fall, and the little trailer that we were staying in became an icebox. One morning we awoke to a small snowdrift piled inside the front of the door. Julie said that she was moving back to her mom's house. I didn't want her to leave, but I understood that this was no way to live. I wanted to move with her, but there was a major problem.

CHAPTER 33 - THE TAINTED HOUSE

Years before Julie's mother had moved into her Wanblee home, a person had been murdered there. The story of how this occurred was told to me like this:

A couple of young men were partying at the house. They had taken some drugs, maybe acid or some other hallucinogen, and were also drinking hard liquor. One of the teenagers hallucinated and saw the other one as a "demon." He panicked, ran to another house and grabbed a bat. He took this bat and went back to confront the demon.

Upon meeting the other boy outside the house, he began to hit him with the bat. He continued to hit his head over and over, until there was nothing left. The blood from this beating drenched the side of the house. Eventually he stopped swinging and was immediately arrested. The victim was dead; his head had been almost completely removed. The police gathered his body parts, and he was laid to rest, but no one ever cleaned the blood off the outside wall. For a long time, the spirit of the murdered boy roamed between worlds.

Later, the mother of the boy who was murdered did a ceremony to free her son's spirit. His soul was released, and the area was no longer "haunted," but because of this horrible event and because his blood was still on the wall, I was not allowed to stay at this house. Even though the spirit of the boy had been freed, there was still an extremely strong negative energy there. Some people would call it a demon.

Once I became a helper in ceremony and started setting up the altar, I became more susceptible to spiritual energies. During the previous summer, I would sometimes stop by this house and visit or take a quick bath. After being there for more than a few minutes, I would begin to feel like I didn't have any energy. If I stayed there longer, I would start feeling flushed and suddenly come down with a fever. The symptoms would normally resolve shortly after leaving the house. At the time I didn't understand why this happened. I didn't know about the murder or that I shouldn't enter this home, but after hearing this story, I understood why.

Grandma explained to me that the boy's spirit was not there, but there is "something" bad there, and as long as the blood remained on the wall, I could not go inside. Grandma went on to say that someone has to wash the blood off with sage water, which would help purify the house. I obviously couldn't do it, and none of Julie's family was willing to.

Luckily, my father was able and willing. One day in early winter, he cleaned the wall and scrubbed it pure again with sage water. He knew this was the only way I could stay with Julie, and he wanted to help us be together. Once he completed this task, I moved in.

A few months after moving to Wanblee, Julie returned from the clinic. She told me with a smile that she was pregnant. I was happy, but also extremely unprepared for this news. I wasn't financially stable, and our living situation was less than ideal. We were residing in a small house that was occupied by three families, with a total of 18 people. I didn't have steady income, so I had no way to support a baby. I began for the first time to think about being responsible for someone besides myself, and I didn't know what to do. Julie, on the other hand, didn't seem worried about it.

My employment at the time was setting up the altar and taking care of the ceremonies. I didn't do this work for money. The knowledge and training I was getting was payment enough for me. Occasionally a sponsor of ceremony would gift me some money, but for the most part, monetary gifts would go to Godfrey. I was comfortable with this arrangement, but it was in no way adequate to support a child. Also, ceremonies mainly occurred in the summer months, but now they were few and far between. My limited income during the summer months had all but vanished. I had to figure how to make money soon. There was still a little time to figure how to get a regular paying job. Now I had to learn more about the town I was living in, and see what opportunities were here.

CHAPTER 34 - WANBLEE REALITY

Living in Wanblee was a new and strange experience. Wanblee contained all the things in life that I needed to avoid. It was full of drugs and alcohol and easy living. There were assaults and open violence on a regular basis. The unemployment rate was at least 80%, and there were limited opportunities for the community members. It seemed that because there was never anything to occupy the younger people's lives, they eventually turned to alcohol and drugs as both entertainment and a mental escape from boredom.

At first I was very wary of people while living in Wanblee. For the most part, I didn't have any trouble with anyone, but there were a few times that I felt true hostility. Occasionally someone would use a derogative or racial slur towards me, like calling me "Custer," but it was rare. The only times that I felt any true danger were when people drank alcohol. At these times, I quickly and quietly made an exit and went to another location. Thankfully, Julie's mother was sober and didn't allow drinking at her house.

Most of the time, I stayed in Julie's mother's house and avoided being out, especially at night. Just walking down the street could be dangerous. There were half-wild dogs that would run barking at you, and sometimes attack if they sensed fear. The young kids of the town would defend themselves against these dogs with sticks and metal bars that they never left home without.

When I did go out, I learned that the town of Wanblee consisted of a few distinct areas. The area where I lived was a group of houses built in the late 1970s. These houses were placed in an unusual horseshoe shape, with residences on either side of the road. There was a large, open space in the center of the housing which contained a basketball court surrounded by tall prairie grass. Most of these houses were in desperate need of repair, and a few should have been condemned.

Besides the area where I lived, there were also three other housing clusters in the town of Wanblee. There was the "old town." This consisted mainly of tarpaper shacks and old trailer houses. There was also the "new" housing that was built in the late 1980s, positioned on a hill overlooking the older housing complex.

The last section of the town was the public school and the quarters for the teachers. Many teachers had to be coaxed into working on the reservation, and the school provided residences for them. In all, there were a few hundred houses and about 500 full-time residents, almost exclusively Lakota.

The home I was living in was one of the most run-down. The doors, walls and ceilings were full of holes, and there was graffiti scrawled everywhere. Some windows were missing, and air leaked in from cracks around the rest. It had three bedrooms, a small kitchen, and a large living area. There was also a full basement.

In each bedroom lived a distinct nuclear family. Julie's mom and her younger daughters lived in one room. Julie's older sister, her husband and their three children lived in another. Julie, Antoine, and I lived in the last room, along with some of Julie's other sisters. The basement was sectioned off with blankets, which became rooms for everyone else.

There was constant traffic in and out of the house, all day and night, with doors slamming shut at all hours. Due to everyone being in such close quarters, verbal fights would erupt, and the house would occasionally explode into arguments. Luckily, everyone really did love each other, so the fights were usually short-lived.

More or less everyone who lived in Wanblee or the surrounding area was in some way related. Relationships and knowing one's family is very important to the Lakota culture. It is a connected way of looking at life that reinforces family ties continuously. Everyone addressed each other by how they are related more often than by their given names. People always addressed each other as Cousin, Auntie, Brother, Sister; or in a way that defined their relationship. It was actually considered somewhat disrespectful to call a person by their name.

I had heard about Wanblee's bad reputation before I moved there. It seemed to be a place where terrible things occurred. Over time, I found that some of this perception was accurate. While living in Wanblee, I began to hear first-hand accounts of abuse and rape. Many of these stories started off as fun parties, where everyone was drinking and having a good time, but by the end of the night someone was hurt or even dead. Some of the stories I heard were so horrific, they sent shivers up my spine.

But there was another side of Wanblee. While living there, I met some of the most warm-hearted people in the world. These people were the types that would give you their last scrap of food and go hungry themselves to make sure you were fed. They were the kind of people that would always give a stranger what they could, from a real place of kindness, not expecting anything in return. They would give even when they didn't have anything for themselves, knowing that the Great Mystery would take care of them. I felt both respect for them and respected by them in their presence. They seemed to truly live from their hearts.

I couldn't understand how there could be such brutality and violence right next to such goodness and living prayer. There was a duality in Wanblee that pervaded all of life. The good and the bad, the right and the wrong, it was all here and lived together. The more each person was in tune with their inner being, the more on the side of goodness they were. Many people I met leaned on their spirituality and traditional culture like a cane, to help them to walk a good path in this life.

This was also what I ended up doing. I came to South Dakota to learn spirituality, and now I was part of the Chipps family, soon to have my own family. I was living in a foreign land, with a foreign culture. I lived in a dangerous place for both natives and whites. I needed the support and protection of the Grandfathers. I needed help to keep myself on a straight path. I began to use spiritual tools and prayers to aid me in being strong enough to live a clean life in this environment. Sometimes, it was all I could do to keep my head above water.

CHAPTER 35 – ANOTHER ADJUSTMENT

After moving into Wanblee that winter, I saw less and less of Godfrey or my family out in the Country. The snow and ice-packed roads prevented frequent travel between the two locations. On top of that, I didn't have my own transportation. When the opportunity arose, I was able to catch a ride from Julie's older sister, but even then the visits were short. After a while, I just stopped trying to go out to the Country unless Godfrey asked for me specifically.

Another reason that I quit going to the Country was the Godfrey had "fallen off the wagon" again. I realized there was a pattern here. During the summer months, when ceremonies were in full swing, Godfrey was able to maintain sobriety for the most part. But as soon as the ceremonies were complete, he began to party and consume massive amounts of alcohol. I wanted nothing to do with this, so even though Wanblee wasn't the healthiest place to live, it was more stable than the Country. My only concern was that everyone living in the Country was staying safe and warm, especially my parents and siblings.

Now that I was living in Wanblee, I was becoming more immersed in the modern Lakota culture. It was foreign to me initially, but I was slowly integrating it into my point of view. I began to truly understand the Lakota concepts of relationship, friendship, humor, living in the moment, and many other cultural nuances.

Over time, I came to really appreciate the Lakota culture and how certain aspects worked, but I could clearly see how others did not. On the other side, I could also understand the "white" concepts of relationship, friendship, humor and preparing for tomorrow. Both cultures had features that were good and healthy, but both also had aspects that were clearly dysfunctional.

I loved the sense of family the Lakota have. Coming from a large family who loved and cared for each other was already familiar to me. What was new to me were the bonds and cultural reinforcement of the extended family and community. Everyone knew how they were related, be it by blood, marriage, or friendship. These bonds were continuously reinforced though speech and behavior.

Friendship also seemed to mean more to the Lakota than what I had witnessed in mainstream America. In the white culture, I saw friends come and go. A friend was easy to find and easy to lose. In the Lakota culture, I saw that when the bonds of true friendship were formed, it was more akin to family. In the Lakota culture, there is a word that people often translate as friend, the word "kola" (ko-la). A kola is more than just a friend; a kola is a companion through the good and bad times, an inseparable partner. This is the Lakota sense of friendship.

In Wanblee, humor was a constant theme in everyday life. Personally, it took me a long time to warm up to it. At the time I was not a very humorous person, and I was bogged down by the seriousness of my work in ceremony. I felt that I didn't have time for laughter. In Wanblee, jokes and subtle humor were entwined into almost every conversation. Everyone was always on the verge of a witty comment that would lighten the mood. Occasionally a humorous event would occur that people would tell stories about for years, and every time the story was told, it would be followed with raucous laughter. To me, it seemed that reservation life was hard, and the Lakota used humor to offset the difficult times that were always just around the corner. After living in Wanblee, I began to appreciate and incorporate humor into my life.

The culture I was immersed in also had a different sense of time. The Lakota seemed to be wholly concerned only with the present moment and not worried about the future; certainly when compared to white culture. The Lakota seemed to find their happiness in the present, often with little or no regard for future consequences. I found this mindset was in some ways very refreshing, and that it brought about a fullness of life that made everything more poignant. Unfortunately, this mindset can also have potentially negative consequences.

Whereas the Lakota live in the moment, mainstream America is always thinking about the future. What I had witnessed and been taught growing up was that I was always to be concerned with the "future." I had to go to school to get good jobs in the future. I had to save money so I could live a good life in the future. I was expected to work all my life in a job I might dislike, just so I can retire in the future. I had been taught to sacrifice my current happiness for some vaguely perceived happiness in the future. I could see that some sacrifices in the present were necessary to make a better life, but I couldn't imagine living a life I hated in the present just to, maybe, have some happiness in the future. This just didn't make sense to me.

Understanding that both cultures had good parts, I did my best to integrate the two, picking what I saw to be the best of both worlds. This was something that I was not only doing for myself, but also in preparation for my child—a child who would be a "half-breed." This meant he/she would also be connected to both worlds, even more than me. I would have to teach this child how to blend the two worlds into a functional way of life. By consciously taking what I saw to be the good from both cultures and applying it to this day and age, I hoped to ensure that not only would I survive and flourish in my current situation, but my yet-to-come would benefit as well.

This led me to a state of mind that was not quite Lakota, and not white, either. It would set me and my child apart, and most likely it would create a type of disconnect with the fullness of both cultures. As for me, I was very willing to see where this path would lead me. As for my child, I figured that this separation would occur anyway, as a result of being a half-breed.

During the time I lived on the reservation, I had already noted certain differences in the way half-breeds and full-bloods acted and were treated. Even in the extended Chipps family, I would hear comments both positive and negative in regard to brothers and sisters who had lighter or darker skin. It was like the children were forced to pick a culture and identify with only one side or the other. I wanted to ensure that my children would know there is good and bad in both, and hopefully I could guide them to the good.

CHAPTER 36 - SACRED SONGS

It wasn't long before my family, including my oldest sister, left South Dakota and moved to Arizona. Knowing how headstrong both my father and Godfrey are, I figured that it was inevitable. I'm sure Godfrey's alcohol and drug use didn't help the situation. My father and Godfrey had a disagreement, and my family left for warmer weather. I had an older brother and sister already living there, so that's where the rest of my family went. My parents offered to take me, but that was not my destiny, yet. I still had much to learn, and I had a child on the way. My place was on the Rez, for better or worse. It was sad to see them go, but at the same time it somehow felt right.

It was at about this time that Godfrey said the Grandfathers prophesized, "That in the end it would just be him and me." I understood this to mean that eventually Godfrey would only have one Helper: me. But right now, Philip was still singing, and I was training a new Helper, a local Lakota man named Waylon.

The winter months in South Dakota are long and frigid. Not many people want to fight the extreme elements to sponsor a ceremony. No ceremonies were scheduled, but occasionally a person showed up requesting one. I had a lot of free time on my hands. During this down time, I decided to expand my understanding of the ceremony songs.

In the past Philip would joke with me about how good I sang, even though I didn't know what I was saying. I decided to correct this shortcoming. That winter, I began to work with Grandma to translate the songs. As far as I knew, this was the first time anyone had attempted to translate the Chipps songs. Prior to that time, a number of them had been recorded, but as yet hadn't been translated.

It was often said by Philip that the songs are the Lakota Bible. All the spiritual information one needs is contained in the songs. I desperately wanted to know what the songs spoke of.

The ceremonial songs are special because they are spirit-given through either a Five Stick, Yuwipi ceremony, Vision Quest or a Sundance. Occasionally, songs are made when someone takes words the Grandfathers have spoken in ceremony and puts them into a melody. Either way, the words come from the Grandfathers, and because of this the songs are sacred. When you sing these words and repeat what the Grandfathers have said, they are drawn to you and will be close by. These songs also contain important information and instructions.

Each medicine family has their own songs, or variations of common songs. The Chipps songs are special in that the family has preserved some very old melodies, and also have songs that are uniquely connected to very powerful forces in the world. Godfrey in the past told many stories of people foolishly trying to copy their songs to gain access to these powers. People had gone so far as to sneak tape recorders into ceremony.

Early one frosty morning, Grandma came to visit me. At this time she was living next door, with Charles' wife, who was our neighbor. She entered in a swirl of misty snow, stomped her feet and shook the snow from her black shawl. The cold air rushed past her, chilling me as she shut the door. The sun had only recently risen, and most of the house was still asleep. Julie's mother had already put on a pot of coffee, so I got Grandma and myself a cup. From the cabinet, I took down a pack of cookies to dunk in our coffee. We both drank the steaming brew and visited, as we often did in those days. She talked about the Commodity eggs and cheese she had for breakfast (supplied monthly by the U.S. government) and how cold the walk here was.

Soon, our conversation turned to more sanctified matters. We talked about the ceremonies and, more importantly, the songs. I told her that I needed to learn what the songs were saying in both Lakota and English. She agreed that this was very important, and she agreed to help. I couldn't have asked for a better teacher. Years ago, Grandma taught the Lakota language for the public schools on the reservation. We decided to start the translation process that evening after dinner.

That night after everyone ate and the children had been put to bed, we waited until the house quieted down. Most of the younger kids had already fallen asleep. The frigid wind and snow whirled outside, rattling the summer screens that had become dislodged. Grandma and I sat at the kitchen table. The only other people awake in the house were quietly watching T.V. in another room. I laid open a green cloth journal on the table to take notes on. This journal was one of the few possessions I still owned that made the trip from Massachusetts with me. The rest of the stuff I had carried in the backpack had been lost or stolen—including the backpack. The notebook was blank, but soon it would contain some of the most important information I'd ever written.

We started with the first song that I learned years ago. Grandma asked me to sing a song the way I understood it. I sang it the way I had heard it, not knowing where one word began or ended. I started with the sweat lodge four directions song.

I sang the song. Grandma softy repeated the melody to herself, after she recognized which one it was. She said the words to the first sentence: Kola howayin tka yace namaron ye (cola ho-wha-yen' tah-kah yah-chay nah-mah-kun- yea). "Friend, I'm going to send a voice, hear me." I would then ask her to repeat the words slowly, one at a time. She said with a smile "Kola… not the cola you drink, but it sounds the same way. Spell it with a K not a C, ha-ha!"

I repeated the words back to her and said "Kola. What does that mean?"

Grandma answered, "It means 'friend.'"

I then asked more specific questions about the Lakota understanding of the word and how it related to the sacred song. "What kind of friend, whose friend, where is this friend from?" Grandma would often be able to explain the Lakota concepts behind the words in greater detail. Sometimes, there was no deeper explanation.

I wanted to make sure I wasn't misunderstanding the Lakota concepts by assuming the way I understood the word was the same way a native Lakota would. I had to get into the mind of a native, and not impose my own predispositions and culture on the songs.

By this process, I began to understand Lakota history, culture, and spirituality much better. I also came to understand that there are huge differences between the Lakota language and the English words we use as translations. We did our best, and over the course of the winter we translated over forty songs. Once we were done, I could sing the songs, pronounce the Lakota words correctly, and also know what I was saying.

In the end, we had a collection of some of the most powerful Lakota songs ever given to humankind, fully translated into English. The translations do not do the songs justice, but it was a start. Over the years to come, I would often refer to these translations to help me remember the deeper meanings behind the words. Eventually I turned this book over to Godfrey, and he refined the translations even more.

The first song we translated was the Chipps' Four Direction Sweat Lodge Song. Grandma explained that there are spirit beings in each of the directions. Seated in positions of authority and power are the Tunkan Oyate, the "Stone Nation People," who have helped us and our ancestors live upon the Earth. These are our friends who spiritually guide and protect us in our lives as we fulfill our sacred purposes. To them we send a prayer, asking for their help.

Sweat Lodge Four Direction Song

> *Friend, I'm going to send a voice, hear me*
>
> *To the west there is a black stone that is my friend*
>
> *To the north there is a red stone that is my friend*
>
> *To the east there is a yellow stone that is my friend*
>
> *To the south there is a white stone that is my friend*
>
> *Above, the Spotted Eagle is my friend*
>
> *In the Earth, the Mole is my friend*
>
> *Friend, I'm going to send a voice, hear me*

CHAPTER 37 -PHILLIP PASSES

In the spring of 1993, Philip was returning from the Rosebud reservation one morning when the vehicle he was driving crashed. The car drifted into the ditch and flipped over an embankment. He was conscious when the ambulance arrived, so they rushed him to the Rosebud hospital. Once he arrived at the hospital, he said his vision suddenly changed, and he knew he was dying. The nursing staff said he sang his death song, went unconscious, and passed away.

This hit everyone hard—it was major shock. Philip was a warrior of the highest caliber. He was a survivor and had beaten the odds time and again. We all knew that he was suffering both physically and mentally due to his paralysis, but we still believed he had a long life ahead of him.

Philip had a fighting spirit in him, a warrior's spirit that always rose to the challenge. In his eyes, one could see the spirit fire burning bright. He never backed down in defending what was right. He loved his family, his people, and his culture so strongly, it shined through in all his actions. In his presence, a person could still see the mystical warriors of the past, defending and protecting their beloved culture and Nation. If Godfrey had inherited the spirit of Woptura, then surely Philip had inherited the spirit of Crazy Horse.

From Philip, I learned how to sing with my entire being. Philip had taught me not just to sing a song, but to become the song. From him I learned to be the voice rising to the heavens. He taught me that we have to go beyond just repeating the words; we have to be sacred singers. To be a sacred singer, our entire beings must resonate with the vibrations of the music, and through the sacred tones we become the prayer.

In this way, a singer become an instrument of prayer—like the drum, the Canupa, the altar, and the Medicine Man. A sacred singer cries out to the Great Mystery and to the Grandfathers, speaking for those who can't speak for themselves. Through our song, we ask for continued help, guidance, health and happiness for the entire world. Philip taught the true meaning of ceremonial song. Philip was a sacred singer.

Philip was an also anchor for Godfrey and often a lone voice of reason. Philip wasn't just Godfrey's brother; he was also his best friend. Philip had been the protector and defender of the ceremonies and his brother his entire life. His passing left a hole in everyone's heart, and he is sorely missed to this day.

We buried Philip at the Chipps' family cemetery. He was laid to rest on the right side of his father, Ellis. On his headstone, there is an engraved poem that Philip wrote years before his death. It speaks of change and life:

THE SPIRIT OF LIFE MAKES WAY FOR ONE ANOTHER

WHERE THERE SEEMS TO BE AN ENDING THERE IS A BEGINNING

EVER ALIVE AND EVER CHANGING

THE GREAT SPIRIT CREATED THINGS TO BE THIS WAY

FROM THE SEED CAME THE TREE OF LIFE

WHAT OF THE ANIMAL KINDOM THAT KNOWS NOTHING OF DEATH

ONLY ANOTHER LIFE TO BE LIVED

AFTER WE'VE LIVED THIS ONE THERE IS NO SUCH THING AS DEATH

THE GREAT SPIRIT MEANT IT TO BE THIS WAY

PEACE

CHAPTER 38 -GRUELING DAYS AND NIGHTS

It was a few weeks after Philip's passing before we began to have ceremonies again. Philip's death was such a devastating blow to Godfrey that he ceased to do ceremonies for a time. He withdrew from everyone for a while.

When we did start ceremonies again, I was now the lead singer as well as the altar boy. Luckily, Philip and Grandma had been excellent teachers. I knew the songs and what they meant. I could clearly pronounce the words and sing the tunes.

Over the years, I had slowly taken on more and more duties in the ceremonies. At first I had started with tending the sweat lodge fires. Then I began to assist in preparing the Hocoka and serving the food. Soon I was being asked to lead the sweat lodges. Godfrey then began to have me set up the altar. I started tying Godfrey and laying him down before the altar. After that, I had learned all the ceremonial songs. Next I was helping put people on Vision Quests. I was taught how to gather and prepare the medicinal herbs and roots use to cure the body. Now, almost solely, I was taking care of the entire preparation and cleanup of the ceremony.

A typical day in which we would have a healing ceremony would be like this: I would wake up about 6 or 7 in the morning, eat breakfast and catch a ride out to the Country (I still didn't have my own vehicle at the time). Once there, I would talk to the sponsors of the ceremonies, making sure they understood what they were to do, and how specifically they were to prepare the offerings. Then it was time to go the sweat lodge to clean out the old stones and air out the lodge by raising the covers. I would stack the first sweat lodge fire, which usually consisted of 25 to 30 stones. If there wasn't enough wood for the fires, I would have to find someone with a vehicle to take me to the creek to cut dead trees. Then it was time to check on the sponsor and answer questions, making sure they were doing their work correctly. I usually asked the sponsor's family or one of Godfrey's daughters to clean the ceremony room and mop the floor with sage water (this was done daily).

The first lodge fire was lit at noon, and I tended it for about two hours. More often than not, Godfrey would have me pour water for the men's sweat lodge. Then the women's sweat lodge fire had to be stacked, lit, and tended for two hours. While the women were in the sweat lodge, hopefully there would be another man available to watch their door (basically just open and shut the door when the woman asked). This would give me enough time to eat something and finish cleaning the ceremony room.

After the women finished their sweat, more stones needed to be heated for steaming the ceremonial offerings, and the people, later that night. I would also start checking with the sponsor to find out how much further until the offerings were completed. If they were slow, Grandma or I would help them finish preparing their tobacco ties and flags. Once all the offerings and food were ready, they were steamed and smudged, and then arranged in the room.

Finally, just before I set up the Hocoka, I would check in with Godfrey to find out if there were any last-minute instructions and if "We're good to go?" Upon his say-so, I would enter the ceremony room, smudge myself thoroughly and begin setting up the altar. Because I was the only one setting up the entire Hocoka, I had to adjust the order. I would set up the altar only to the point of pouring the mole dirt on the altar board, and then arrange the outer flags and tobacco ties. After the outer area was completed, I would return to the altar and finish its construction.

The altar preparations were halted just before the Canupa was loaded. I'd exit the room and round up all the participants and Godfrey. The hot stones, cedar smudge and a bucket of water were also fetched. Everyone would meet outside the doorway of the ceremony. Each person was steamed and smudged as they entered the room. Everyone would take their seats in the appropriate locations. The people would again be smudged, this time by sweet grass.

I would take my seat before the altar and signal to Godfrey that the altar was ready to be completed; he would start singing the Canupa loading song. I quickly drew a special design on the dirt, then taking pinches of tobacco mixture and passing it through cedar smoke, it would be offered to the Grandfathers. Then I picked up the Canupa and repeated the offering process. The loaded Canupa would be carried over to Grandma and handed to her.

Godfrey prepared himself to be tied, removing his shoes and shirt. He would stand at the opening of the Hocoka, facing away from the altar. I would bind his hands behind his back with a sinew cord. The blanket would then be thrown over him, and a rawhide rope was used to tie him. He was turned and laid face down before the altar, with the assistance of a few other men. We would take our seats outside the Hocoka as the lamp was blown out. I'd lead the singers in the songs that were needed for that night's ceremony. At times, I would instruct the sponsor or the rest of the people to say their prayers out loud.

Once the ceremony was complete, the lamp was lit and the Canupa was smoked. After the last man smoked the Canupa, some of the ash from the bowl would be spilled on the altar. A small pinch of bread was then smudged and placed on the mole dirt as a food offering. The altar would then be taken down, and the electric lights turned on. The food was passed out and eaten.

After the meal, the dirty plates and cups were smudged and collected. Any leftover food on people's plates was gathered together to be buried later. Everyone would say Mitakuye Oyasin one at a time, all around the room. I would exit the room first, and everyone else followed. Once everyone left, I would clear the leftover food and garbage out of the room, and then take the spirit plate up to the graves. Then it was time to catch a ride home. It was usually well after midnight by the time I arrived back at Wanblee.

This whole process was repeated day after day, sometimes for weeks. Often I would recruit people to help with the tasks that needed to be completed throughout the day, but sometimes no one was there to help. It was grueling and tiring, but the Grandfathers sustained me.

I was overwhelmed with all the work, and at times made mistakes. The hardest part was making sure the sponsors and the attendees were doing what they were instructed to do. There was a constant barrage of questions that had to be answered, often repeatedly. I learned great patience and how to multitask to the point of extreme efficiency. It also taught me how to deal with many different personality types, yet it was a continual struggle to rise to the challenges day after day after day.

CHAPTER 39 - TRAGEDY

Late that spring, Julie was ready to give birth to my first child. Julie's mother and I took her to Pine Ridge hospital, in the town of Pine Ridge. She was told by her doctor that the baby had to be delivered by Caesarian section, because that's how Antoine had been born.

We arrived at the hospital on a stormy morning on June 7th. The hospital was a large yellow brick building on top of a hill that overlooked the town of Pine Ridge. It was an older structure, built in the 1920s. Originally the hospital had been run by the Catholic Church. With the overcast skies, the rundown, dirty yellow building had an eerie look to it and an ugly aura. I sensed it was full of ghosts.

Julie signed in and was immediately prepped for surgery. She was whisked off, and within minutes our daughter, Alicia, was born. She was a beautiful baby with a full head of black hair. Julie's mother and I visited the baby for a while, until Julie awoke in her room. The baby girl was brought to Julie, and we followed. She was happy to have a girl, and I was happy everyone was healthy.

Julie and Alicia had to stay in the hospital for the next three days. The baby stayed with her mom while she recovered from the surgery. The nurses told me I could not stay, and besides that, I knew Godfrey needed my help with ceremonies. I returned back to Wanblee ... and back to work.

On the third morning after Alicia was delivered, I woke up excited. Julie and the baby were coming home! I took a bath and got dressed in the best clothes I had. I wanted to look good for their homecoming. I still didn't have a car, so Julie's mother took me out to the Country. From there, Godfrey, a family friend, and I were to ride to Pine Ridge together.

When I arrived, it was still early morning and everyone was drinking their first cups of coffee. There wasn't a cloud in the sky, and the morning air was cool but comfortable. I decided to wait outside for Godfrey, I couldn't sit down anyway. I was anxious to get going, but everyone else was moving like cold turtles. Finally, Godfrey got his boots on and came outside.

He seemed distant and wasn't saying much that morning. I was still pacing in circles, waiting to leave. Godfrey came over to me and said that he needed me to take care of some things. He got real quiet and looked off into the distance. He said, "Sal, I need you here. You have to fix the sweat lodge."

My jaw dropped. I didn't know what to say. I was getting upset, fast. I thought, "Why wasn't I going? Couldn't the sweat lodge wait?" Before I could ask any questions, he jumped in the car, and he and his friend sped down the driveway. I stood there, stunned, and watched the dust of the vehicle disappear in the distance. They were gone.

I felt really bad that I wasn't going with them. Sometimes I just couldn't understand Godfrey. It seemed like he was heartless. I asked myself, "Why is he going and not me? This is my daughter, and I have a right to be there." In anger, I said to myself, "I bust my ass day and night for him, and then I get left behind!" I felt like I couldn't have a life outside what he wanted, so I stomped off to the sweat lodge area.

There was a friend and a Helper out in the Country at this time, named Gary. He had been helping me prepare the ceremonies over the past few weeks. As I walked up to the sweat lodge site, I saw that he had already begun to prepare the area. The old willows had been removed and burned. Gary was a hard worker, and the site was ready. We now needed to drive in to an area in the Badlands to cut willows to rebuild the sweat lodge. At this point, I really didn't feel like talking to anyone, so I just said, "Let's go."

We left for a stand of trees that grew in a creek deep in the Badlands. There were a few ways to get there, but we took the long way. I wasn't in a rush. We hardly said a word on the drive. We passed through Wanblee, and then turned onto a gravel road leading down to the creek. Gary asked why I wasn't picking up Julie and the baby, and I truthfully answered "I don't know."

Once we arrived at the willow stand, I went off by myself and began to cut down the saplings. I was offering tobacco and praying as I took the life of these trees, but I was still upset. After trudging through the mud and cutting 20 trees down, I began to just accept the situation. There was nothing I could do about it now, anyway. Over the years of working with Godfrey, I had come to see that sometimes he asks people to do things that, at the time, don't make sense or seem fair, but there usually is a good reason for his request. I started to believe this was the case in my situation.

We finished cutting the willows and tied them in a bundle. With some effort, we managed to hoist this bundle onto the roof rack of the truck and secure it in place. Gary asked me if I would like to drive home. I said, "Sure." I started feeling a little better on the way back. I was hoping Julie and the baby had made it to the Country by now.

We had just pulled up to the junction where the gravel road meets the pavement, when off in the distance I heard the wail of a siren. An ambulance with lights flashing and sirens blaring flew by as we stopped at the intersection. I didn't think much of it, but they sure seemed in a rush!

We pulled onto the pavement and headed for the Country. The ambulance was speeding off in front of us in the distance. I noticed it turn off the pavement, and begin traveling down the gravel road that goes past the Chipps' property. Suddenly, my heart dropped. I had the overwhelming sensation that something terrible had happened. I felt sick in the pit of my stomach. I hit the gas, speeding up to catch up with the ambulance. Gary grabbed onto the dash as we flew over the rolling hills. I hardly hit the brakes as we crossed the wooden bridge near the Country, and we went airborne. Gary said, "Don't kill us!" I didn't care.

The ambulance stopped on the road on top of a hill at the far northwest corner of the Chipps property. The lights on it were still flashing as we pulled up to one of the worst car accidents I'd ever seen.

The hill where the accident occurred is so steep that people in a car on either side of it can't see what's coming until they are at its apex. As a rule, on this section of the narrow dirt and gravel road, cars going in either direction occupy the center of the road. What had happened was Julie, Godfrey, and Alicia, in the car driven by the family friend, had come over the hill just as a pickup truck with a female driver and two kids came up from the other side. The vehicles collided head-on at a high rate of speed. The cars then bounced back about 50 feet. Looking at the damage to the vehicles, I knew this was bad.

I slammed the truck in park and jumped out of it. Godfrey was standing on the side of the road, supporting his right arm. He looked banged up, and his wrist was deformed. I saw two people in uniform, which I assumed were the Emergency Medical Technicians, running around the scene. I heard moaning coming from within the pickup truck as I passed by. I immediately went to the car Julie was in.

As I approached the passenger side of the car, I heard someone yelling from the ground near the driver's side door. The door was open, and the family friend was lying on the ground. I never saw him, but I could hear him calling out for someone to help the baby.

That's when I saw Alicia lying face down on the front passenger seat. She had a bluish tinge to her skin, and she breathed only in occasional gasps. I put my hand on her back and said a quick prayer. I knew I shouldn't move her, so I ran to the ambulance. I looked in the door and told the EMTs that the baby wasn't breathing. I could see that there were already patients from the other vehicle in the ambulance, but one of the EMTs ran out and grabbed Alicia and took her back to the ambulance.

I went to Julie. She was still sitting in the back seat. Her head hung down like she was semi-conscious, but occasionally she began to speak and pray out loud. She seemed to be in a daze, not knowing where she was. I noticed a long cut on her shin, down to the bone. I sat with her and tried to keep her still and calm. She would be silent, and then suddenly begin to pray to the Grandfathers at the top of her lungs, only to become silent again.

After what felt like hours, another ambulance pulled in. They took Julie and put her on a backboard and strapped her down. The first ambulance soon left toward the nearest hospital in a town called Martin. It took Alicia, the family friend, and the driver of the other car. I stayed with Julie and rode with her in the back of the second ambulance. Godfrey also was transported in it.

When we pulled into the hospital, the staff unloaded Julie and her dad. I saw the two EMTs from the first ambulance standing by the entrance. The female EMT was leaning against the wall, smoking a cigarette. She was crying. I walked over to her and asked how the baby was. The EMT wiped her tears and said she couldn't say anything; the doctor would let me know. I walked into the hospital.

It was chaos, with the hospital staff running everywhere. This hospital had only a one-bed emergency room. They were understaffed and unprepared for this many critical patients. I found Julie still strapped to a backboard in a room down the hall. There was a woman with her, making sure she was still breathing. I went over and held her hand. She was still only semi-conscious.

After a short time, the doctor walked in. He put his hand on my shoulder and told us that Alicia was dead. He said that she died before she made it to the hospital, but they tried to revive her. A chaplain placed his hand on my shoulder and asked if we would like to pray. I couldn't answer. Tears streamed down my cheeks.

Julie and Godfrey ended up being flown 100 miles away to a larger hospital in Rapid City. At Martin, we were told that the drivers of each of the vehicles and the baby had died. The children in the pickup were fine and released from the Martin hospital that night.

All of the Chipps family and myself immediately departed for Rapid City. We understood that Godfrey had fractured his arm and he needed surgery. Julie was going to be assessed to make sure there weren't any other injuries. We arrived in Rapid City at dusk.

Julie had already been cleared and was waiting for us at outside the Emergency Room. She still seemed dazed, and was sitting in a wheelchair in a hospital gown. Godfrey was in surgery and would have to spend the night. The doctors told us Godfrey would never be able to use his right hand again, but they didn't know the power of the Grandfathers. Julie's mother rented a motel room that night so we could all get some rest. I collapsed on the bed and fell asleep crying. During the night, I woke up once. Someone in the room was sobbing; I think it was Julie's mother.

The next morning when Julie woke up, she asked her mom where Alicia was. She kept saying it over and over again. "Mom, where's Alicia?" Her mom just cried and said she was gone, that she died in the car accident. During the night, Julie's senses had come back to her, and she finally understood what had happened. She began to scream and cry, until her tears ran dry.

Godfrey was released that day, and we all returned to Wanblee. Now we had to prepare for a funeral, the second one this year.

Prayer Song

> *Look towards the west, our Grandfathers are coming*
>
> *Sparks of light are coming.*
>
> *Above there is a man who is painted red, you said he would have powers.*
>
> *When is it going to be?*
>
> *Above there is a Spotted Eagle, you said he would have powers*
>
> *When is it going to be?*
>
> *If he shows his shadow he will be seen, you said this*
>
> *I am having a hard time.*

CHAPTER 40 -DEATH'S LESSONS

Within the week, we held a wake and funeral for Alicia. Many people from all over the U.S. attended and paid their respects. My family did not. They stayed in Arizona because they were having a difficult time financially, and there was still a certain amount of tension between my father and Godfrey. Truthfully, I was grateful that they did not come. I knew that they would want me to leave and go to Arizona with them, and this was something I was unwilling to do.

I wasn't going to run away. I had a mission and goal here; learning spirituality and incorporating it into a lifestyle. I was going to complete this goal no matter what. On top of that, Julie needed me now more than ever. I couldn't abandon her. It was very difficult burying Alicia and not having the support of my blood relatives, but I knew I would make it through and be far stronger for it in the long run. For now, I just had to get through one day at a time.

Lakota wakes and funerals are very involved. The Chipps' extended family, along with most of the community, came together to help with the funeral. The wake was held at the local Community Action Program Center (CAP Office), the only building in town that could accommodate a wake at the time. It was an open-casket wake that lasted three days. There were extensive prayer services, Lakota songs, and feasts. Over the course of the wake, everyone was given time to mourn and start healing from this tragedy. No one was rushed, and everyone was allowed to show their grief.

Julie was still in shock. She spent her days in a wheelchair, still recuperating from her injuries which made it painful for her to walk. She had to take some strong analgesics as well.

I mainly sat in the back of the room. I felt disconnected from everyone and everything. I was so emotionally overwhelmed, I just shut down. I hardly talked for two days; only once during the entire wake did I have a long conversation with one of Julie's cousins. It was a very lonely time. One day, I got up and went to the Country to dig the grave. The digging was all done by hand, with shovels and muscles. I felt terrible digging my own daughter's grave, but it gave me time to mourn in my own way, and the exercise was therapeutic.

Alicia was buried at the Chipps family cemetery. She was interned on the left side of her great-grandfather, Ellis Chipps. Her headstone reads:

ALICIA RAE ANN GENCARELLE-CHIPPS

JUNE 7-10 1993

WE LOVE OUR LITTLE ANGEL

After the funeral, we had a "Giveaway." A Giveaway consists of giving out many gifts in honor and remembrance of the deceased. From the time of Alicia's passing to the time of her funeral, different items were collected for this event. There were quilts and blankets, cigarettes and tobacco, towels and many other useful and necessary items. There were also beaded jewelry and other native crafts.

After Alicia was buried, everyone gathered for a final feast. Once the feast was complete, the Giveaway began. Certain people were honored for their help with the wake and the funeral. The cooks and the cleaners, the Lakota singers, and the priest were among the people that were given star quilts. Star quilts are highly prized by the Lakota, because the eight-point star represents the Morning Star and the White Buffalo Calf Woman.

The Giveaway made everyone feel good; both those who received and those who gave. It helped heal both the family and the community, emotionally. To me it was on odd sensation to have such grief and also such happiness at the same time.

The loss of my daughter taught me more about death than I ever wanted to know. I hadn't really seen death before on this level. Prior to the car accident, I had never witnessed anyone die. The closest I ever came to death was when I had attended Philip's funeral, and one of my grandfather's funerals back in Massachusetts.

My grandfather was in his eighties and had lived a long, full life. Philip had been suffering from his paralysis, and his life had been restricted. In both cases I could see that death was a release from suffering. This made sense to me. But Alicia's death didn't, and it was far more personal. She was only three days old. She was innocent. She wasn't sick and hadn't lived out her days. I began to ask, why did she die, and what is death?

This forced me to contemplate death. I began to understand that death was closer than I had ever realized. I now saw that death was a part of life, one of the most important parts. I came to understand that we are all born to die. Death is everyone's ultimate destiny. I also came to realize that death was also ever-present and could come unlooked for…and unexpected.

As I contemplated this, I looked around and saw that life was both beginning and ending at any given moment. I saw how much life it took to just to sustain me; all the food that I consume each day to live in this world. It seemed to me that humans take the death of the plants and animals for granted, though we hold our own life in high regard. Just driving down the road, how many bugs do we kill? Are their lives worth less than ours? Is it any less traumatizing for the deer dying on the side of the road than a person who was struck by a car? I came to understand that all beings tremble before death.

To me, this was an important revelation. From that day forward, I tried to hold all life in the same respect that I give people. I tried not to kill without a good cause, even accidentally. Wasting food became a terrible sin. I saw it as being careless and disrespectful with other beings' lives, which ultimately is disrespect to the source of all life, the Great Mystery. I even tried not to swat mosquitoes. If I did have to kill, it was done with prayer.

I also contemplated the afterlife and what happened to our spirits after death. Even before this experience, never did I believe that death was the ultimate end. As far back as I can remember, I believed that there was "something" beyond our physical passing from this body. Through prayer, I came to understand our spirits continue, and there are many possible places for our spirits to dwell.

Even now I didn't fear death, but hoped it would not come for me until the completion of my work in the physical world. I did begin to fear for the loss of loved ones. I didn't ever want to experience that type of pain again. I pray every day for my children to outlive me and grow to be old men and women.

After our daughter died, Julie and I grew closer, bonded together by our grief and loss. Our relationship grew stronger, and within the year she was pregnant again. This time things went better. Our second child, a son, was born on June 15th, a year after the accident.

For the next four years, we sponsored memorial dinners for Alicia. As part of each dinner, we also had another Giveaway. Each year during the memorial dinner and Giveaway, the pain of our loss lessened and our hearts were slowly healed. As we fed the people and gave gifts in memory of Alicia, our heartache was replaced with joy, until by the fourth year the traumatic events of her death were just a vague memory.

Julie and I eventually had three sons together, Anthony, Salvatore III (Yamni), and Adrienne. Each one has blessed our lives, and has brought everyone great joy and happiness.

Our children are a special gift and blessing from the Great Mystery. They are sacred, and must be raised with love and taught how to live upon the Earth in balance. Raising children has taught me more about people and myself than any other experience. It has given me insight into the circle of life and beyond.

CHAPTER 41 - CRYING FOR A DREAM

Later in the same year that Alicia passed away, I Vision Quested for the first time. I felt weakened by the pain in my heart from the loss of Alicia. I needed to find my center again and strengthen my spirit. I hoped to gain the guidance I sought by communing directly with the Grandfathers and the Great Mystery.

My quest was to be completed in a vision pit located on the Chipps' property. It had been dug by Horn Chipps himself. Horn Chipps was the originator of the Yuwipi Ceremonies as we know them today. He was instrumental in transitioning the medicine from the old nomadic Lakota culture to the modern area. Horn Chipps was a bridge that ensured the medicine would continue, and the ancient teachings would not be lost. Within the ceremonies and songs, the prehistoric knowledge and understanding of the physical and spirit world is still preserved. The "modern" Yuwipi ceremony, as Horn Chipps first created it through spiritual guidance from the Grandfathers, contains all this information.

These ceremonies are like a map that holds all the knowledge of the natural and spirit world, knowledge that used to be an everyday part of Lakota life. Just like a map, it shows us a path back to our origins. The information and the power contained in this ceremonial format was shared by Horn Chipps when he helped to create seven other Lakota medicine men. From this source, the medicine first spread through the Lakota Nation, and then the United States, and now the World.

I was honored to be allowed to enter this pit for my first Vision Quest. The vision pit is a six-foot deep hole dug into the earth, with stairs cut into the wall. Willows form a dome over the pit, and these are covered with tarps and blankets. A vision pit provides protection from the elements, and more privacy than one done out in the open. For my first quest, I went in the pit for one night.

Due to my years of helping vision questers, the preparation was easy. I already knew what I needed to do. Everything was quickly prepared the day of the quest, and I was ready to enter the pit at dusk after purifying in the sweat lodge. During the night, I prayed for help and health and happiness. I had many waking dreams. Some I remember, others I do not.

I had a Vision of Alicia in the pit, which I never spoke of until now. Late that night, I was sitting down on my bed of sage, wrapped in a star quilt. My disheveled head hung low in fatigue; my grip on the Canupa kept slipping, as I had become so weary of holding it upright. My mind was in a stupor and wandering, until abruptly the darkness of the pit was gone, and I found myself sitting in a field of golden, sun-soaked grass. I was sitting there in this field with my blanket wrapped about me and the Canupa still clutched in my hand.I It was as if I had been transported to another time and place.

Over a hill came a Native American family. One man was on horseback pulling a travois, with a couple of other people walking alongside. They approached me and walked in a circle, I noticed a baby wrapped in a blanket riding on the travois. The family circled me, and in my mind I knew the baby was Alicia. The family completed the circle and walked back the way they came. I sat there in the field and prayed with my tears for the baby I lost. I prayed for her to be well in her new life. I begged her new family to take good care of her, and I sent my love to her with all my heart.

Through this vision of Alicia, it became clear to me that she had been born only to live with us for a short time, and teach us lessons. Her death brought about many changes in my life, all for the better. I also knew now that I had the power to prevent this from happening again.

Many people who were not directly involved with the ceremonies believed that Alicia's death was somehow related to mistakes that occurred in ceremony. After praying about this during my Vision Quest, I came to realize that this was only partially true. The ceremonies are just a spiritual reflection of the physical world, sped up and empowered by the medicine.

The backlash from making mistakes in ceremony occur no differently than the backlash from making mistakes in the physical world, except that the repercussions occur faster, and can be more intense. The principle is basically the same in both worlds. Alicia didn't die because of something that occurred in ceremony. Alicia died because of events that played out in the physical world. There were many, many incidents that led up to her death—and yes, some were related to ceremony, but the vast majority of the precursors to this tragic event were people's issues in the physical world.

At sunrise, Godfrey got me out of the pit, and I purified in the sweat lodge.

It was after this Vision Quest that I began to realize what a "vision" really is. Up until this point, I had only imagined what it was like to have a vision, and this was based on other people's stories. I came to realize that a vision is a dream. Once I recognized this, I saw that people have visions all the time.

There is a part of our minds that holds a doorway to the spirit world. Any time a person sleeps, daydreams, or uses their imagination, they are tapping into this source. This is our personal connection to the unseen world and all its possibilities. In everyday life, we can control and manipulate this gift. Even while reading this book. Imagining these events unfolding is a type of vision.

The difference between a daydream and a vision is that during a Vision Quest, we create a sacred space through our preparations and offerings. When we construct a Hocoka and enter this sacred space, setting aside all that it takes to live in this physical world, we are granted protected access into the spirit world.

During our quest, we sacrifice food, water, and sleep, and become like a spirit. Once we enter the Hocoka and "Cry for a Dream" with a strong, unselfish purpose, the Grandfathers hear our prayer and provide direct guidance. It is then that we have sacred dreams.

I had just done a one-day Vision Quest and received much. I couldn't imagine what a four-day Hembleciya would be like. Someday, I would find out.

One thing I noticed was that many of the answers to my prayers came to me after I completed the quest. I had expected that during my night in the pit, I would have great revelations, but that just didn't happen, so I initially felt like I had somehow failed. It wasn't until the follow days, weeks, and even years that many of the questions I had asked were finally answered. I began to notice all the many ways in which prayers were answered. This led me to another realization.

I prayed to Wakan Tanka, the Great Mystery, and to the Grandfathers. The Great Mystery is all of creation, something beyond what humans know or can perceive. The Grandfathers are guardian spirits, energies, and the powers of this world and the universe. The Grandfathers are intermediaries between humans and the Great Mystery. It's similar to a Catholic praying to the saints, or to Jesus. The Grandfathers are just on a different level, so to speak, so they have different connections to creation.

I came to see that if the Great Mystery is the foundation of creation, and all things both seen and unseen are from this source, then when we pray to the Great Mystery via the Grandfathers, we are really praying to all of creation.

What this means is any part of creation could answer our prayers. When we send out a prayer to the Creator, creation will respond to us in the best way for our situation. Our answers could come in the form of an animal, a person, a book, a song, or an infinite number of sources. It is our job to be vigilant and be aware of creation, so we recognize the answers that we are given.

When we recognize the answer to our prayer, it is like a circuit that is completed and allows sacred energy to flow. When we pray and open our minds to all of creation, we will "hear" the answers, which then allows us to continue to pray and be grateful. This is a circle that continually moves the energy of prayer, both around us and through us.

This also explains why the ancient people paid particular attention to animals, often taking them as signs or omens. I had been taught that animals are considered pure. Due to this purity, they have a special connection to the Great Mystery. It is believed that from this connection, they are often used as messengers. If a person sees an Eagle, it means good luck. White Owls hanging around a house are messengers of death. This is just part of some of the ancient understandings that people who lived close to the Earth have.

Over the years, I found that people who have become unbalanced often lose their ability to "listen" to creation. They usually still have the ability to ask for help, but they have become deaf to the help when it arrives. Thinking that they were never heard, they continue to ask. Sometimes they become disheartened and lose all faith.

It reminds me of the story of the preacher and the hurricane. As the story goes, there was a violent hurricane approaching the coast where a preacher lived. He was a man of faith and knew God would take care of him, so he prayed. While he was praying, he heard the local government order an evacuation over his radio, but he thought, "No, I will pray for help, and God will take care of me," so he stayed in his home. As the storm approached, the police went door to door, making sure everyone evacuated. The police advised the preacher to go somewhere safe. He then told them, "No, I will pray for help and God will take care of me." Finally, when the hurricane hit and this man's house began to flood he retreated to the rooftop. A rescue helicopter came to him and lowered a ladder, but again this man said, "No, I will pray and God will take care of me."

In the end this preacher drowns and goes to heaven. He stood before God and asked, "Why did you let me die? Didn't you hear my prayer for help?" and God answered, "I did hear and I did try to help you, three times. I sent you a message through your radio, then I sent the police to your house, telling you to go to safety, and finally I sent a rescue helicopter, but you refused my messengers."

CHAPTER 42 -PERSONAL TIME TO GROW

During the following years, I continued to help with ceremony and continued to learn and grow. I also continued to Sundance, and ask for knowledge and guidance in my life.

Over the years, we ended up traveling all over the country. Godfrey had wanderlust in him; the nomadic lifestyle was still living on in a new form. We traveled from coast to coast, doing ceremonies and going where the Grandfathers guided us. Winter months were spent in warmer climates, and summers were spent back in South Dakota. On many occasions, we traveled where we were needed, meeting many good people.

Our travels eventually lead us back to Massachusetts. We stayed at a house located in the foothills of the Berkshire Mountains, about 45 minutes away from my childhood home. There were 14 of us in all; Godfrey, his wife and four young children, a few of his older children from his first marriage, Julie, myself, Antoine, and our 2-year-old son, Anthony. We all stayed together in a nice house with a backyard that butted up against the woods.

There was a beaver dam just behind the house that formed a small lake, just big enough to put a canoe in. I ended up losing my glasses in the beaver pond one chilly spring day, while trying to paddle the canoe. It capsized, throwing me into neck-deep freezing water. My glasses flew off my face and were never seen again. Antoine, who was about 5 years old, laughed from the shore as I scrambledf out of the water. Standing there freezing and dripping wet, all I could do was laugh with him.

It was during this time in Massachusetts that I decided I could no longer set up Godfrey's altar. A mistake occurred that caused this chain of events.

A local person that also worked as a part-time Helper passed out the ceremonial water, starting with the wrong person. It was an obvious mistake, but I didn't catch it in time. Godfrey was angry and told me if any more mistakes happened, that my son Anthony would die.

Initially, this statement shocked me to the core. The pain of losing Alicia was still fresh in my mind, and Godfrey's words were like a knife that cut open a scar on my heart. I was not willing to risk my child dying for anyone. I knew as soon as the words passed Godfrey's lips that my apprenticeship was over.

I came to realize that this was a blessing, and it forced me to the next stage of understanding. Over the past years, I had been fully inducted into the ceremonies and Lakota spirituality. I had learned all the techniques of prayer, healing, and information-gathering that I had been seeking. I knew it was now time to step out on my own and fully utilize what I had learned. Godfrey's statement spurred me forward and forced me out of my ceremonial rut. I knew I had to stop being an "altar boy." It was time to walk another path.

Up until this point, I had no problem with taking on the responsibility of the ceremonies. Over the years of helping, I watched as people came asking for spiritual help, after years of abusing themselves and others. They came looking for something or someone to save their lives after they had made a mess of them, and had become so sick that there was nowhere else to turn. I was expected to help them find a new life, sometimes at the sacrifice of my own. I knew this was part of my job and accepted that, but I could not be expected to sacrifice my child's life. Godfrey's statement was completely unacceptable to me.

After Godfrey made the proclamation about Anthony dying, I continued to set up the altar for a short time. Over the next few nights, I prayed for the people to be healed, but I also prayed and talked to the Grandfathers about my situation. I told them that I didn't want to set the altar up any more. I stated my concerns and reasons, making it clear that I wasn't turning my back on them and I still believed, but I couldn't put my family at risk like this.

I asked to be released from helping in ceremony and setting up the altar. Even though I did not want to help directly with the ceremonies, I still wanted to continue on this spiritual path. I promised the Grandfathers that I would pray with my Canupa every day. I promised to pray for Anthony and for all my family each day, no matter what. This was my way of showing my commitment and continuing my education. I was not turning my back on the Great Mystery or the Grandfathers; I just wasn't willing to put my family in peril.

Without ever having to say a word, Godfrey knew what I was praying, and he wasn't happy. It was not long after I began to ask to be released from setting up the altar that he left Massachusetts. He left me, Julie, Antoine, Anthony, and a few other family members there at the house. We had no car, no job and no way to pay for rent. Living in Massachusetts like this wasn't going to work. Julie called her mother and asked for help. Her mother was able to raise money, and within the week we had bus tickets for South Dakota.

I personally was hesitant to go back. I was unsure of the direction of this new path and wanted to be sure I went in the right direction. I originally had gone to South Dakota to help with ceremony, and now that was done. I considered going to my relatives in Arizona, but after talking to my father, I felt that would be a mistake. I discussed my concerns with Julie, and we eventually decided that South Dakota was the best place for our family.

Once we arrived back in Wanblee, I kept true to my commitment, praying with the Canupa every day. This wasn't always easy, especially living back in Wanblee. We were staying at Julie's mother's house again, now with over 18 people under the same roof. I couldn't pray inside, so I ended up going behind the house to a small stretch of prairie that I would stealthily sneak off to. During the summer months, the tall grass would provide me some protection and privacy.

Throughout the winter, however, I would have to go out well before sunrise to not be disturbed. Winters in South Dakota are brutal, with temperatures dropping to below zero and relentless attacks of winds, rain and snow.

Even though there were houses just a few hundred yards from where I sat, it felt like I was very isolated and protected. I would pray either in the early morning or late at night to avoid detection. I found that I particularly enjoyed praying at dawn; facing east and watching the stars slowly fade away as the light of the new day became brighter.

It was during this time I noticed that the most profound occasion to pray is in the pre-dawn hours, right around four a.m. This is the time of night when the rest of the world sleeps. It seemed like I had the Grandfathers' undivided attention. I prayed for hours at a time and asked many questions. My understanding increased, and I felt blessed. Many nights, I would watch the Morning Star rise in the east, followed by the dawn of a new day.

I had been told the Morning Star is an eagle feather upon a sacred being's head, the Sun. Even now, the Grandfathers were strong in my life. My break from the role as a Helper and student of ceremony provided me with time to reflect and grow. My growth now was sustained not by my role in ceremony and Godfrey's tutelage, but directly by the Canupa and the Grandfathers. I was taking my education to the next level.

The Grandfathers communicated to me in many ways during this time. While sitting in the prairie, Canupa in hand, many new and wonderful insights would come to my mind. Often, upon completing my prayer, I would return home and take a quick nap before the start of the day. After praying one night, I had a dream that was so vivid, even fifteen years later I can still recall all the details.

In the dream, I was Sundancing at the Chipps' property. I was all by myself, pierced to the tree and facing west. As I was dancing, the Tree of Life began to lean over, and I became frightened. I felt weak, and the energy drained from my body. I could barely lift my feet. The tree wilted and the sky darkened.

Then, from the family cemetery, I heard someone singing. I looked up to see an old man dancing down the hill. He was dancing supported by a cane, and singing as he came toward the Sundance grounds. He entered from the west gate and quickly approached the tree. He placed his hands on it, all the while singing and dancing.

The tree began to straighten and stand upright again. The sky cleared, and the sun shined through the clouds. The tree budded and new leaves grew and rustled in the wind. The whole tree glowed, and I felt new life flowing into me again. I was renewed and full of energy. Now I joined this old man in song and dance. The man danced back up the hill to the graves and was gone. When I awoke that morning, this Sundance song was echoing in my mind, and I knew everything would be all right.

Sundance Song

> *Do you want water?*
>
> *Do you want water?*
>
> *There is no water!*
>
> *There is no water!*

CHAPTER 43 - RECONCOLIATION

The year passed quickly, and eventually Godfrey and I reconciled. He had just returned from a long journey across the United States when he called Julie and asked to see us again. That evening, we met out in the Country and hugged. I was happy to see him, and we made our amends.

It did not take long before Godfrey asked me to help in ceremony once more. I was hesitant to get involved again. My relationship with Godfrey and the ceremonies had changed. I was no longer the neophyte, needing a teacher to show me the way. That path ended over a year ago in Massachusetts. Now I had stepped into my own power and had a deep relationship with the Grandfathers through the Canupa. If I came back to ceremony, it wouldn't be as a pupil. It would be as a Helper with knowledge and authority.

Godfrey knew I was doing something that would benefit the ceremonies and his work; I was walking with a Canupa. This is no easy task in this day and age. My motivation was my love for my family, especially my children and the generations yet to come. This love is what kept me walking out to the prairie during the winter to pray, even when it was tens of degrees below zero. Love is the most powerful motivating force in the universe, and Godfrey needed this power, the ceremonies needed this power, the sick and the dying needed this power. Even before Godfrey and I were reunited, I knew he would ask me to become a Helper once again and contribute my love to the world.

Also, I was no longer concerned with the previous threat against my family that had been uttered in anger. By using my Canupa and praying daily, my family and I were provided a level of protection that would shield us from negative energies. The Canupa empowered my prayers for protection and wrapped us in security. It was like a blanket that covered and warmed us against the bitter negative and destructive forces. I knew my children and family were safe. I could not say the same for anyone else, though.

Godfrey did ask me to set up the altar, and knowing that this time it would be different, I agreed to help.

After that, every day I would take time in the afternoon and walk down to the creek near the ceremony house. There, I would sit in a grove of cherry and ash trees and make ties and load my Canupa. First I would pray for children and the generations yet to come, and then my family. I would also pray for the coming ceremony. These prayers helped and guided me, and the ceremonies went very smoothly. I was happy, and so was Godfrey.

It had now been over seven years since I helped create the Medicine Wheel garden back in Massachusetts. Many things had changed over the years. I had changed and had grown from a 15-year-old boy to a 22-year-old man. I had grown physically and spiritually. Now I even had a family and children of my own. With the Grandfathers' help, I was transformed from a passionate kid with dreams of spirituality into the primary Helper and son-in-law of one of the most powerful Lakota Medicine Men alive. Many of my ideas and misconceptions had been wiped clean and replaced with deeper understandings. Ignorance was replaced with knowledge and humble prayer. So much had changed.

One thing had remained consistent through all these years: the symbol of the Medicine Wheel. From the creation of the Medicine Wheel garden until the present, this symbol has been a reoccurring theme in my life. It seems to hold a deep and special significance for me.

In the Lakota tradition, the Medicine Wheel is a circle with a cross inside. The circle and cross are painted four different colors: black, red, yellow, and white. It is one of the most common and easily recognized Native American emblems.

I saw this symbol everywhere. It was on shirts, billboards, and in books. It was part of every ceremony that I attended. The circle with a cross seemed to be a message that held many secrets. I often wondered at its significance beyond the obvious. I hoped to understand what it meant to me.

Many people offer interpretations of what the Medicine Wheel means to them. There are other tribes besides the Lakota who use various forms of the Medicine Wheel, each with its own symbology. Some of the meanings placed on the Medicine Wheel are different, some even contradictory. I decided to learn directly from the Grandfathers what this meant to me, and how I was to approach it. I was blessed to be granted a unique view of the power behind the Medicine Wheel during one of my many Vision Quests.

Through the quest, I came to understand how these colors and the circle represent various aspects of human life. I was shown that the colors represent four different stages that all people go through in their existence. This is what was revealed to me:

The black is the beginning of our journey. The black represents the potential new life that grows within the darkness of a womb. It also represents the mind of an infant that is newly born, a mind that is ready to be filled with all the experiences that this life will bring—experiences that will help educate this infant into becoming the person that life demands of it.

Red is the next step in the path. It symbolizes the young child, so full of life. At this stage, the child knows only of life, and has no concept of death as yet. Children at this stage live only in the moment; everything is new and fascinating. They experience life to its fullest, one instant crying with all their heart, the next laughing and playing without a care in the world. Children at this stage still have a strong connection to the spirit world and will occasionally speak of things far beyond their years.

Yellow is the third stage. It represents the adult and the mind that is aware of consequences. At this stage, a person knows of good and bad, right and wrong, life and death. The adult is fully engrossed in the physical, sometimes forgetting the potency of the spirit. The Yellow phase is one of knowledge, when the mid-point of the circle is reached. From here, one can see the path just traveled and perceive what lies ahead. The highest physical potential a person has is reached during this phase.

White represents the human entering back into a state of purity, in preparation to return to the spirit world. The mind is purified and the mistakes of life are balanced. Even the hair of a person turns white to show what is happening. Eventually the person leaves the physical world and returns to spirit, merging with the purity of that world. And the circle continues.

At the center of the circle is a cross. The cross represents choice. During life, each person must make choices that will decide how they move around the circle of life. The cross meets the outer circle at the intersection of each color. This represent the points of reference that a person can make the choice from. At the center of the circle, the two paths intersect, connecting all four colors and states of mind. This is the place of balance and true vision, a place where choices *should* be made.

I saw that the four phases of humans are not four individual steps with a line drawn between each color, but a gradual transformation where one color slowly changes to another. In each phase, a person has certain qualities that are distinct to that stage, but they also carry aspects of their previous stages. The pathway is not a straight line, but a circle without end, one life leading to the next. Certain aspects of previous lives may be carried into the future.

From this vision, I understood that every decision at each stage of our lives has consequences that reverberate throughout the rest of our lives. We all have made a choice to be born into this world and live the life set before us. From there, we have many choices that affect how we proceed around the circle of life.

Because of this understanding, I came to better accept certain tragic events in my life, including the death of my daughter. Julie, Alicia, and I made the choice to live through this experience. This pivotal understanding has led to many blessings in my life and continues to dictate many of my actions, even today. Accepting the responsibility for my choices, even when they resulted in difficult lessons, was the next step in truly taking responsibility for my life.

From adversities come understanding, blessings and new paths to walk upon.

CHAPTER 44 - A NEW PATH

The year passed, and I continued to pray daily, making tobacco tie offerings and smoking the Canupa. In many ways I was blessed and felt complete. One area of my life that always seemed to be lacking was finances. Julie (who was pregnant again), Antoine, Anthony and I were still living in my mother-in-law's house. All of us were living out of one room.

During the winter months, I would work at the local grade school and help teach. The school had a program called the Parent Tutor, where a parent could go help teach their son or daughter for three hours a day and make fifteen dollars. I would walk the mile and a half every day, rain, shine, or snow, just to earn what I could. I enjoyed teaching and eventually began to substitute. I was fortunate this winter because a third-grade teacher took maternity leave, so I ended up teaching for three weeks straight.

I found I enjoyed having money and being able to purchase the necessities of life, and then some. There were many times over the past years that I would go hungry because there was no food, or only enough for the kids. Because of my low income, I did receive free food through the "Commodity Allotment" program. This consisted of canned food, some freeze-dried eggs, and a delicious five-pound block of American processed cheese. It wasn't much, and it wasn't healthy, but it was far better than nothing. We made do with what we had and survived the lean times by supplementing our diet with fresh deer meat. Other family members living in the house qualified for food stamps, and they also contributed their share.

But now that I was making money, I finally could buy enough food for everyone, and also have some left over to get a few personal items. Regrettably, the job at the school was only temporary. But fortunately, someone at the local ambulance service noticed my work ethic and gave me a rare opportunity.

The summer of my 22nd year, there was a knock at the door. Everyone else in the household had left for the nearby towns of Martin or Kadoka. The monthly supply of food stamps had arrived, and it was time to shop. Being the only one home I went to the door and was greeted by a lady I knew from Crazy Horse High School. She had stopped by to tell me there was a First Responder class at the CAP office. She recommended that I go check it out.

After she left, I decided I didn't have anything better to do, so I walked the dusty trail across the housing to the office. I had no idea what a First Responder class was at the time. Once there, I was informed that I would be learning basic first aid. The class had already started, but the teachers were nice enough to let me join the group. With my background as a former lifeguard, I found the material was easy. Over the lessons of the next few days, I learned new lifesaving techniques and skills. I ended up passing the final test with 100%.

It was then that the instructors told me about an opportunity to become an Emergency Medical Technician (EMT). There was an upcoming class that I could attend. It was designed to be a crash course to quickly certify new EMTs to work with the local ambulance service. This class would be held in the town of Pine Ridge the following month. It was free of charge, and books would be provided. The ambulance service would also provide transportation to and from the class. I went home and talked to Julie about this extraordinary opportunity. The class was scheduled to run for eight-hour days, five days a week, over the next four weeks. We both agreed that this was a great break for our family.

The ambulance supervisor in Wanblee supported and encouraged me to take the EMT class. She lived near the path I walked to and from the school, and over the past few years had observed my dedication to the Parent Tutor job. She saw that no matter what the weather was like, nothing stopped me from working. She told me that she needed dedicated people like me to work for her. It was then I noticed she looked familiar. This was the female EMT that I had seen at the accident when Alicia died. She was the one who ran over from the ambulance and picked Alicia out of the car. She was also the EMT who had been standing against the wall at the hospital in Martin, smoking a cigarette and crying.

I was excited to have this opportunity to learn something new. This was a rare opening, especially for a white person on the reservation. Tribal jobs were given "Indian preference," so I automatically fell to the bottom of the list. Luckily for me, the ambulance service was looking to hire more people than they had applicants, so I had guaranteed employment...if I passed. I felt like my prayers had been answered again. It was an honor to have this chance to make a living, and to do so while helping the Lakota people.

The EMT class was being held at the Oglala Sioux Tribal Ambulance Service's central base. This was located at the old Indian Health Services (IHS) hospital in the town of Pine Ridge. It was the same hospital where Alicia had been born four years ago. A new hospital had been built the past year, so the tribal council decided to turn the old building into government offices and a central base for the ambulance service.

The Oglala Sioux Tribal Ambulance Service covered all of the Pine Ridge Indian Reservation, and occasionally responded off the reservation into surrounding communities and into Nebraska. There were four base stations for the ambulances to respond from. The main one was located at the old hospital in Pine Ridge. There were also bases in the towns of Oglala, Kyle, and Wanblee. If I passed the EMT class, I would be working from the base in Wanblee.

The class went by fast, and I graduated with an excellent score. I began to work as an EMT in August of 1996. I remember my first shift like it happened yesterday. I clocked in for my 24-hour shift at 7:00 in the morning. I had on my clean, pressed uniform and shiny new boots. I was ready to work hard and save lives. I had a belief that the people called 911 constantly, and we would work day and night. That proved to be untrue.

All day I paced the floor, looking out the window, anticipating a phone call for help at any moment. By 10 o'clock at night, we still hadn't turned a wheel on the ambulance. I decided to lie down, but just for a minute. I ended up falling asleep with my uniform and boots on, still anxiously awaiting my first call.

Finally, at about 2:00 a.m., the phone rang. The dispatcher informed us that we were to respond to a local residence. When we arrived at the house, a man walked out the door complaining of something in his ear. After placing him on the cot in the ambulance, we took a look in his ear and saw the hind legs of a bug, but it was too deep for us to pull out. We ended up transporting him to the new hospital in Pine Ridge, an 85-mile trip. I was the driver, and my supervisor was sitting with the patient in the back. It was a long drive, about an hour and a half. Upon arrival, the doctor quickly pulled a cockroach out of our patient's ear. He was released within minutes, and we all retuned back to Wanblee.

I asked my supervisor, "Is this how our days usually are?" She answered, "Yep." This was not what I expected.

CHAPTER 45 - DIFFERENT WORLDS MERGE

Godfrey was happy that I was working for the ambulance service. He said it was a good thing, and that someday I could teach others how to save lives. My job didn't interfere with the ceremonies much either. My supervisor and co-workers were all Lakota and most understood traditional ways. I never had to explain why specifically I was coming to work late or getting off early. They knew if I was working out at the Chipps,' it meant I was doing ceremonies. All I would have to do is let my supervisor know I would be a few minutes late because I was "helping out in the Country." She never questioned what that meant.

During the summer, I was always allowed enough time off for Sundance or Vision Quests. Finally I had the money I needed, and I was still able to live this spiritual path.

About a year after becoming an EMT, another opportunity presented itself. I was told that there was a paramedic course I could attend. Becoming a paramedic was a long and involved process, but it would allow me to use the latest lifesaving tools and techniques. This course would take a year, and upon completion I would be one of the first paramedics to work for the Oglala Sioux Tribal Ambulance Service.

I was very nervous about this leap in responsibility and skill level, but I couldn't pass this chance up. Again, the costs of the class would be taken care of, so it was just a matter of me studying and attending class. My supervisor made sure my application was handed in on schedule. She was a big supporter for a second time.

I began paramedic school my second year as an EMT. I found that due to the format of the class and the technical information I was learning, I had to change my thinking processes. After moving to South Dakota, I had left my analytical mind back in Massachusetts, and out of necessity had developed more of an intuitive thought process. The material I was learning now was forcing me to become more analytical again.

The technical information was challenging on many levels. I had to learn medical terminology and anatomy; there were also new pharmacological terms and concepts. Also, I had never been good at math, and it was a big part of the course. Algebraic equations were something that I had all but forgotten over the years.

Even now, through this transitional period of education, I was praying with my Canupa every day. I began to ask the Grandfathers for help with the paramedic course. This was not out of selfishness. After all, I was learning this information to help save lives. Daily I would go off into the prairie and load my Canupa, and pray for understanding. There was one specific time that I really felt the Grandfathers helping with my education.

At various times during the class, all the students had to stay in the Black Hills at a training center near of the town of Sturgis. It was winter and the roads were icy, so we ended up spending a week at the training center learning hands-on skills. We learned how to insert IVs, how to administer medications, and how to put a tube in someone's windpipe to help him or her breathe. At the end of this week, all the students had to take a mid-term exam. If I was to continue, I would have to pass the test with at least 80%.

I was struggling with portions of the course, and I needed to get my mind wrapped around the material. I could not quite understand some of the information I was reading in the books. I decided to ask for help from the spirit world.

The night before the test, I went out into the snow-covered pine forest in a section of the Black Hills that was near the school. There was a full, bright moon, and it shed light on my path into the woods. The snow reflected the light and gave everything a mystical, silvery glow. I walked up a hill until I found a level area among the pine trees. Looking out to the north, not too far away, I saw Bear Butte illuminated by the moon. This is a very sacred butte to many of the northern plains tribes. It was massive and impressive in the moonlit sky. I sat facing it as I loaded my Canupa.

Once the Canupa was filled, I started to pray, as I had so many times before. Prayers for help with learning the material to become a paramedic were said. I sat there in the woods, cross-legged, holding the bowl of the Canupa while resting my forehead against the stem. I began to feel something—there was a funny tingling sensation in my head. It almost felt as if my brain was moving, like it was rearranging itself. I knew the help in understanding I was asking for was being granted.

I lost track of time as I sat there, but after a while I felt the cold chilling me and knew it was time to go. I smoked the pipe and said my thanks. I left that hillside with confidence that I would succeed in my task.

The next day, I easily passed the test and was allowed to continue onto the final phase of the course. After that night on the hillside, the entire course became easier. From that point, on my mind became more analytical and adapted back to learning and working in "western mode." I hoped to blend this new way of thinking with the one I had learned in ceremony, so neither part of my mind would be diminished. This blending of the two minds has been a challenge over the years, and at times conflicting, but it has also given me two directions from which to understand medicine.

The ceremonies had taught me that the most important aspect of a human is his or her spirit. A person's spirit must first be healed before any true health can be attained in the body. This was proven to me time and again over the years of helping in ceremony.

In western medicine, the spiritual aspects of a person aren't even acknowledged. Because the spirit isn't measurable by our medical instruments, western medicine considers it unimportant to the current condition. The health of the spirit is not a paramedic's concern. We are only taught to deal with the physical problem at hand, and leave the "spiritual stuff" to the clergy.

Without imposing my own beliefs on my patients, I have often included silent prayers during my treatment of patients in the back of the ambulance, hoping that in the short time I spend with them, they will receive a blessing; Most of the time, they do.

CHAPTER 46 - CALLED TO THE HILL

My job as a paramedic was bringing in a steady flow of income. At first we weren't used to having so much money. We ended up spending it on a lot of unnecessary items, and Julie liked to splurge the rest on Bingo. When I first started working, we were living in a "feast or famine" state of mind. In the past we had become accustomed to having either nothing or excess. Back in those days, when we did have money, we just spent it as fast as we could because it wasn't going to last. With all the families under one roof, there were many mouths to feed, so the little money that we did have was spent swiftly.

Now, after working for a few years, it became apparent that this mindset was not the best way to handle our current financial situation. Eventually we became accustomed to having a continuous source of income and started to manage it better. I finally was able to purchase my own car. The freedom that money provided was completely new and exciting to us at the time. We started to look for a house of our own.

A year after becoming a paramedic we moved into our own house in Wanblee. It had been Philip's house, and after his passing it went to Julie's older sister. She eventually moved out, and we moved in. We had the money it took to live on our own, and we were making the best of it. It was nice to have a home of our own, even though there was a lot of damage to the structure. We moved in during the late winter and immediately went to work repairing what we could. The windows and doors needed to be fixed, and there were holes in the sheet rock that had to be patched.

After the job was complete, I used the extra sheet rock to turn part of the basement into a ceremony room. It was a quiet place to pray and have some alone time.

Just before we moved in, Julie gave birth to our second son, Salvatore III. I had been named after my grandfather on my father's side of the family, so technically I was Salvatore II. Julie wanted to name this child after me, but I resisted. Having two people in a house with the same name can get confusing. I also didn't want any of my sons to compare themselves to me that way. We ended up compromising. I agreed that he could be Salvatore III, as long as we called him Yamni, which means "three" in Lakota. It was an appropriate name, because he was Julie's third son and my third child. A month after he was born, we moved into our new home.

Later that year, Godfrey called. It was now early summer, and there was a group of people coming out for a Vision Quest. There were six people in all. Most were old friends. Godfrey said that he needed to meet with me out in the Country to talk. Julie, the kids and I loaded into our car and drove out right away.

Godfrey met us with his usual smile and hugs. He explained to me about the group of people on their way for a Vision Quest. I was thinking that he was going to ask for help putting them on the hill. Instead, he said I also had to go on a Vision Quest—a four-nighter! He said, "Son, it's time for you to do this. The Grandfathers said that this is something you have to do."

I was excited, but also nervous. Julie, on the other hand, seemed very worried. I felt I was as prepared as I could be at this point. In many ways, I had been preparing for this quest since that day years ago in Massachusetts, when I first heard about Vision Quests. Over the last ten years, I completed all the physical and spiritual tasks that led me up to this point. The subsequent step was to actually do it. We started purification the next night.

We purified for four days. There were seven "questers" in all. We prayed together and asked for help and guidance. We all set out to complete this task, but we were all very uneasy. To go without food, water, or sleep for four days and nights seemed impossible. From my previous experiences of vision questing, I had an idea how hard this would be. During the four days of purification, we prepared our offerings and ourselves for the task ahead. Our hearts, minds, bodies and souls all had to be completely ready for this undertaking.

On the morning of the fifth day, the seven questers and Godfrey awoke at daybreak. A Canupa was loaded, and we stood together in a line facing the dawn of a new day. It was a beautiful day and a warm morning. We greeted the rising sun with prayer. Still groggy from a fitful night's sleep I stood there praying for the best outcome possible. It felt like I was on the edge of a cliff and about to jump off. In my mind, I decided to focus just on what needed to be done in the moment, and forget about the future.

After greeting the sun with prayer, the final preparations were started. We needed to make our four-hundred and five tobacco ties and our prayer flags, gather sage, and purify all these items. This was all completed before noon. My location for this Vision Quest was to be on Eagle Nest Butte. A few years back, a man had dug a vision pit on the east side of the butte. That was where I would spend the next four nights. I drove to the butte and got as close to the pit as possible, but there was still quite a climb to get the rest of the way there.

Once I arrived at the pit, I arranged all the offerings quickly and with prayer. The prayer flags were placed in their directions. A special offering of red wool cloth, a shell button, and an eagle plume were placed between the black and red flags. The ties were strung about the bottom of the pit. A new Canupa was also offered to the Grandfathers. This was hung from the willow frame at the top of the pit. The floor was covered in sage. Canvas tarps were used to cover the top of the pit and doorway. Everything was set. I smudged the area with sweet grass and returned to the Country.

There, we had a final feast. Normally for a one, two or three-night quest, a person doesn't eat or drink the day of the quest, but on a four-nighter, a person is allowed one last meal. I ate sparingly, because I'd been restricting my diet for the past few days in preparation for the lack of food that I would be enduring. What I did eat provided me with a much-needed energy boost.

The day wore on, and evening was fast approaching. We assembled at the sweat lodge for the final purification. A sweat lodge fire was started. Next, our Canupas needed to be loaded. New tobacco, osha root, and red willow bark was combined right there at the lodge. In this way, we made the mixture that would be placed into our Canupas that night. A new knife was used to cut up the ingredients. The amount prepared had to be the exact amount it took to load our individual Canupa—no more, no less. They were then loaded while offering every pinch of the mixture to the Great Mystery and the Grandfathers, asking for help, and for our prayers to be heard.

We then entered the lodge. The stones were brought in one at a time. Each stone was touched by a Canupa, and cedar needles were sprinkled on it. The lodge filled with a sweet-smelling smoke. We joined together as we sang the commitment song, pledging ourselves to our quests.

Commitment song

> *Come here*
>
> *I am going to speak in a sacred manner*
>
> *My relatives and I will live*
>
> *As I cry, I am sacrificing myself*

This was followed by a special four directions song, the Vision Quest Four Direction Song:

> *They put these on me, they put these on me*
>
> *They put a Black Plume on me*
>
> *I'm sending a voice to a Black Stone*
>
> *They put a Red Plume on me*
>
> *I'm sending a voice to a Red Stone*
>
> *They put a Yellow Plume on me*
>
> *I'm sending a voice to a Yellow Stone*
>
> *They put a White Plume on me*
>
> *I'm sending a voice to a White Stone*

We said our prayers. Many people cried for help, while some were silent. We were sacrificing ourselves for our relatives. We were all willing to die so that future generations would live in health and happiness. It was a big honor to sit among people that held others' lives above their own. Next, a song was sung that explained the offerings made to the Grandfathers during a Vision Quest.

Vision Quest Prayer Song

> *Someone from the heavens said this*
>
> *"Give me the Canupa one at a time"*
>
> *"Give me the Eagle Plume one at a time"*
>
> *"Give me the Red Wool Blanket one at a time"*
>
> *"Give me the Shell Button one at a time"*
>
> *"Give me the Tobacco Bundles one at a time"*
>
> *Someone from the heavens said this*
>
> *See me*

It was time to take our final drink. This was done by taking a bundle of fresh sage and dunking it in the bucket of water. From this bundle, we drank whatever water we could get. This was repeated four times. I noticed on the first drink that if I tried to suck too much water out of the bundle, the taste was bitter. By the fourth drink the smell of fresh sage enveloped me; more refreshing than the water in my stomach. Before exiting the lodge, we were reminded to give up all it takes to live in this world: no eating, no drinking, no sleeping, and to keep our eyes closed. We were to be like spirits that have already passed out of the physical world.

We exited the lodge. One at a time, we crawled out of the doorway backwards. As we did so, a Helper wrapped us in our star quilts. This would be our only protection from the elements for the next four nights. The night air mixed with our bodies' perspiration and chilled us. The Helper guided us to car that would take us to our individual Vision Quest locations.

CHAPTER 47 -ON THE HILL

It seemed like a long drive to the butte, and it was a difficult hike up the rise with my eyes closed. The Helper guided my steps and took me to the doorway of the vision pit. By the time I entered the pit, I could tell it was well into the night. I quickly took my place at the center and stood on the sage.

There I remained. I stood until my legs grew tired, then I sat until I became sleepy, then I would stand again. This was repeated over and over throughout the night. By the first morning, I was exhausted. Time became a blur at this point. Slowly, my consciousness began to change. I would drift off into waking dreams, only to quickly come back to my prayer. I tried to remain as focused as possible. Eventually the waking dream won, and I began to drift off into a vision.

I saw my life play out before me. I imagine this is something similar to what people see when they have a near-death experience and "see their lives flash before their eyes." But what I saw wasn't my life "flashing" before my eyes. Instead, it was passing very slowly.

The first vision was of my birth. At first I didn't even recognize who was being born, but as the scene played out I realized what I was witnessing. Then I watched myself grow and start experiencing the world around me. The vision showed my interactions play out in clear detail. I viewed my life as I grew into a boy through all the events that I experienced. It was like standing outside my body watching a movie about myself.

Oddly enough, I didn't feel any emotions or connection to the events I was observing. It was like I was watching a story about someone else's life. The vision continued, and I grew into a young man. I watched my meeting with the Chipps family and Godfrey. Soon I was helping with ceremony. Finally, the past few years of my life played out before my eyes. The story of my life ran right up to the point of me entering the pit, sitting there having a vision of my life.

My mind was unexpectedly back in the present moment. During this vision, I noticed that from the age of about 15, when I had my "awakening," I had lived life with a very narrow focus. My entire existence had been almost exclusively in the pursuit of spirituality. Now I was 25 and I realized that my life over the past ten years had been dedicated to what I thought was the most conducive way to learning spirituality. Over these past years, I had tried not to "sin," not to make mistakes, not to do or be around "bad things." In many ways I had tried to live as a saint, and at times I succeeded.

Suddenly I noticed that my legs ached from sitting so long. I had to stand! My legs were numb, so I braced myself against the wall of the pit. After standing there a few minutes, my strength returned, but it was temporary. Soon I had to sit down, and again a waking dream came upon me.

In my next vision I saw an old, weathered stone monastery on top of a high hill. I saw monks living at this location that had cut them off from the rest of the world. They isolated themselves in the belief that if they lived a life full of prayer, sacrifice, and dedication to God, they would be closer to the Truth. As I looked upon these monks, I could relate to their desires and beliefs. I felt some kinship to them but, upon looking closer, I came to realize that even though these monks were still in the physical world, in a way they were already dead.

They lived like spirits, with little true connection to the physical world. They grew old and died and never truly came to understand the material world they were a part of. They never learned who they were, and why they were given this life to begin with. I became aware that in many ways, I was doing the same thing. I was cutting off and isolating myself from the world, and in a way, cutting out a big chunk of my life.

Through this vision, I understood that I had spent so many years focused on learning about the unseen world, I had very little insight into the physical world. In that moment I decided that I needed to understand the material world much better. I needed to connect with the Earth in a deeper way.

I understood that the world as we know it, at this time and place, is unique, and will never in all of eternity be repeated again. All the opportunities and blessings that this planet holds, in this moment, are fleeting and not going to last forever. In this moment of understanding, I decided to learn and experience more of what my humanity holds. I knew that I needed to learn the lessons of the physical, as well as the spiritual, to become a complete human being.

Now that I realized how much I had missed during my pursuit of spirituality, my next pressing concern was, "What if the Grandfathers gave me Powers? Would I be conflicted between what I needed to do in ceremony, and how I needed to interact in the physical world?"

I now understood that I wasn't ready to take on the commitment needed to work with the Grandfathers on a higher level. I began to say prayers to the Grandfathers and to the Great Mystery, telling them that I wasn't ready to carry the Medicine. I said that I needed to experience this world first, both the good and the bad, to get a better perspective on life. I promised that I would return after I had come to a better understanding.

The quest came to an end on the fourth morning. A Helper climbed the butte and took me out of the pit. I was happy to have completed my commitment, and happy to have survived. I had not abandoned my quest or come off the hill early, as I saw so many people do in the past. I remained in prayer and kept my eyes closed on the drive back to the Country. Once there, I was guided in to the sweat lodge, where Godfrey waited. We steamed off with hot stones, and I told him what had happened on the hill. I'm not sure what he thought. He didn't say anything.

After exiting the lodge, I found out that I was the last quester to return from the hill. Everyone had already purified and had gathered to partake in a feast. Julie, my sons, Godfrey and Grandma were there. Grandma and Julie had made toast, eggs, and bacon. Grandma also brought us fresh fruit. It tasted better than any fruit I ever ate, before or since. The morning light was bright and clear, I felt renewed, like this was the first day of a new life. It was good to be alive.

CHAPTER 48 -LEAVING THE REZ

Over the next years, I continued to help with ceremony, but we began to expand our horizons. Julie, my children, and I would often travel up to Rapid City during my days off from work. At first it was just day trips to shop. After a while, we started staying overnight at motels. Eventually, if I wasn't working on the ambulance or doing ceremony, we spent all our time in the city. Soon I wanted to live closer to the city and enjoy the opportunities it offered.

Adrienne, my third son, was born the spring of 2000 at Rapid City Regional Hospital. He was Julie's last child. All her children had been born by Caesarian section, and the doctors advised that she should not have another one. After Adrienne was delivered, an operation was performed so Julie could not get pregnant again. I was glad to have another son, but I think Julie really wanted a girl before she stopped having babies.

After Adrienne was born, we decided to move closer to Rapid City. I was tired of living in Wanblee. We spent all our free time in the Black Hills, anyway. And I had never really wanted to live in Wanblee—it just worked out that way. Now that I was working and making some decent money, I could finally leave and take my children to a better place.

In 2001, we purchased a house and moved to a town called Black Hawk, about five miles outside of Rapid City. It was a nice house with a big back yard and a creek nearby. Huge cottonwood trees provided shade, and there was green grass everywhere. It was a peaceful place and felt safe. This was like a dream come true to me. Ever since my visit to the Black Hills when I was seventeen, I felt drawn to live there. Ten years had passed, and finally I lived in the foothills of the Paha Sapa (pah-ha sap-ah), the Black Hills.

The move was a big change for Julie, since she was leaving most of her family back on the reservation. I think she resented me for taking her away from her loved ones and the life she had known. Even though it was an adjustment, I knew this would be a better place to raise our children.

The reservation has some very beautiful things about it, but also limited opportunities and a lot of dysfunction. I wanted us to live a spiritual life, not one surrounded by the anger I felt on the reservation. I didn't want my children to grow up thinking drugs and alcohol abuse or violence was normal. They are my future, and they need every opportunity to succeed.

Rapid City was by no means perfect, but compared to Wanblee, it was safer and held more opportunities. On the reservation, I felt like I had to be constantly vigilant to protect my children from all the negativity and pain that surrounded us. Now that we lived in Black Hawk, I felt less apprehensive and could relax a little.

By the time we moved, Godfrey wasn't on the reservation either. A man had been assaulted at the Chipps property. The assault was being investigated by the FBI due to the Major Crimes Act, which gave the federal government jurisdiction over certain serious offenses committed on the reservation. Godfrey already had a criminal record, so he had become the prime suspect. He was now on the run and living in different parts of the country. Before he left, he told us that he was going to turn himself in as soon as he was done with his ceremonial commitments. He had healings to do, and loose ends to tie up before he went to jail again.

Over the years, Godfrey would keep on a straight path during the summer months, praying and doing ceremony almost continuously — but during the winter months after the ceremonies stopped, he would start drinking, often heavily. That's when I would try to distance myself and my family from him. I loved Godfrey as my father in-law and my teacher, but I couldn't be a part of his weakness.

The alcohol abuse worsened year after year, and finally came to a head with this assault. The assault was bad, bad enough for the FBI to get involved. I really didn't know what happened that night, and really wanted nothing to do with it. I felt bad for Godfrey and believed that he wasn't completely responsible for what happened, but he was taking the brunt of the accusations. I knew at some point he would be taken to jail for a long time. My only hope was that his time in jail would give him the opportunity to address his alcoholism.

This entire situation was terrible, especially because everyone involved was family. One of my brothers-in-law had already been arrested and sent to prison because of this crime. The FBI had questioned Julie and me about the incidents that night, and they were watching the entire family in hopes of catching Godfrey. Part of the reason I moved my family to Black Hawk was to get away from this craziness.

I didn't want to get caught in the middle of this criminal investigation. This was not what I had signed up for. I had come to South Dakota in support of the ceremonies and to help people live in health and happiness. What I was witnessing was not health or happiness. In fact, it was just the opposite. I wanted no part of the abuse, neglect, or continuous cycle of violence that pervaded reservation life.

The recent events of the assault and having the FBI knock at our door forced my hand. I had to get us away from this downward spiral. We moved out of Wanblee as soon as the house in Black Hawk was purchased.

Even after the move, I continued to pray as always. The connection to the Great Mystery and the Grandfathers is in our hearts, not just the land in which we reside. My children and I eventually built a sweat lodge in our back yard. We put up a six-foot high fence around it so there would be some privacy from the neighbors. The fire pit was dug deep into the ground and covered with a spark deflector. I didn't want to upset the neighbors, so I took the necessary precautions to prevent them from knowing what was going on behind the fence.

My children were getting older. Antoine was eleven and was a good help. Anthony was six, and Yamni was three. Adrienne was still crawling around in diapers. The older boys would help stack the wood for the sweat lodge fires and get things ready. They all loved to sweat, and would often wrap up in towels and wait by the lodge long before the stones were ready.

The boys were also learning the sacred songs. They were each finding their own voices. Sometimes it was like singing with a bunch of yelping pups. Normally we sang the songs quietly, but on one occasion my old friend Gary stayed with us for a few days, and we sang like we were back in the Country. I think he forgot that we now lived in a place surrounded by white people, some that didn't care for "Indians" too much. I'm guessing that we scared some of the neighbors that day.

Our life at this time was good, and we had all we needed.

After a few years, the law caught up with Godfrey and he was arrested. I became very concerned for our greater family's future. Godfrey had held everyone together through ceremony. Now that he was incarcerated, there was no one left that could fill his shoes. I wanted to make sure that these traditions continued, even if just among my relatives. I decided that it was time to go back up on the hill and finish what I had started on my last Vision Quest. I still had a promise to keep.

Prayer Song

>*You who walk with altars, come here.*

>*You who walk with altars, come here.*

>*I'm having a difficult time, take pity on me, help me.*

CHAPTER 49 -TO THE HILL... AGAIN

I began to prepare for the Vision Quest in late June of 2005. I had the sweat lodge at my house, so I purified there. All the items I needed were gathered from the abundance of the Black Hills. On the final day of purification, my family and I traveled back to Wanblee. Upon arrival, I went to Eagle Nest Butte and finished readying the vision pit. The pit was covered with tarps, and I made sure I could climb the stairs cut into the earth.

The next day was spent preparing the offering and mentally preparing myself to enter the pit that night. For this quest, I wanted to be pierced to the four directions so I asked one of my brothers-in-laws to help me with this. I met him on the butte late that afternoon before going into the pit. He cut me and placed two wooden skewers in my chest, and two in my back.

After that, I hugged and said goodbye to Julie and my sons. I entered a small sweat lodge that had built near the vision pit. There, I purified and sang the sacred songs. Upon exiting the lodge, I wrapped myself in a quilt, walked over to the pit, and closed the door. This would be my home for the next four nights.

Cedar posts had been planted in the intra-cardinal directions, and a rope with a loop on the end had been attached to each post. These loops were attached to the skewers in my back and chest. The ropes were just long enough for me to sit down, but did not allow me to slump over. This would ensure I didn't fall asleep!

The first night was grueling. By the early morning, my legs were shaky when I stood. I had decided to break one piercing every night, just before dawn. This morning I broke the piercing that connected to my right chest. My head spun, and I began to feel like there was a hollow space within my chest. This was a new and very odd sensation.

Suddenly, it felt like my spirit left my body. I was quickly traveling somewhere, as if being pulled to some distant location. I ended up standing before a giant man sitting on white stone floor, with four white pillars holding a roof high above his head. He was a huge being that appeared to be human, but looked like the result of a person who never stopped growing for thousands of years. He was enormous.

I asked him who he was and what to call him. He replied with a booming but gentle voice, "I am what you would call father." I responded to this by saying to him, "You know why I am here." I said, "I seek the power to help all people at the most, and my family at the least."

He answered by saying, "You already have the power. I have placed it here."

As he spoke these last words, his enormous hand reached out and pointed to my chest. His long fingernail went painfully through my spirit body, and waves of energy radiated out through me. My spirit glistened with many colors and light as the energy flowed through me, like the sun reflecting off rippling water.

I then asked him for guidance on how to use this power. His answer was that soon, I would be shown how.

Unexpectedly, I asked a question that I hadn't even considered until that very moment. I asked, "Of all the religions in the world, which one is the right one?" He gently replied. "The one that worships me."

I thanked him for the help and guidance, and was suddenly traveling backwards. My spirit reentered my body. I was abruptly back in my physical form, feeling dazed.

Over the next days and nights, the hollow sensation in my chest increased. I felt as if the person I was, my "ego," was fading away, and in its place, energy from the spirit world was pouring into me. As this energy filled my being, my internal vision became my reality. The walls of the pit vanished, and in my mind's eye I looked out upon the clouds and across the heavens. Many spirits came to me during that time, and I heard words, many words, spoken in Lakota that I could not comprehend.

During one of these days, a light beam shined upon me from above. I didn't see it, because I still hadn't opened my eyes, but I could perceive it and feel it. It was as if a concentrated beam of sunlight shined down from the heavens beyond the covers of the pit. This light penetrated right through the top of my head and through my skull; I could feel its warmth in my brain. In my mind I heard a voice say Lakota words, and felt a sense of peace and love that I can't put into words. Then the light beam was gone.

I didn't know what the words meant, so I began to repeat them over and over. I had to remember them and ask Grandma what they meant. I intuitively knew this was a name given to me by the spirit world; the name I was called on the other side.

By the third night, I was beyond exhausted. I had not slept for three days straight—the piercings had worked at keeping me awake. I felt like I would drop at any second, and I couldn't do anything to prevent it. Over the past nights I had broken free from two of the four piercings. Each time I broke, there had been a sudden rush of energy that sustained me in a conscious state. Breaking free from my third piercing tonight was my last hope in remaining awake.

I tried to stand but collapsed to the ground. I tried to stand again and again, but each time, my legs gave out and I fell to my knees. My legs were so shaky that every muscle fiber violently quivered. Finally, I got to my feet, my knees literally knocking together. The piercing I wanted to break was on the left side of my back, so I began to lean forward. I was holding the Canupa and praying for strength. My flesh tore loose and I fell, crumpling to the ground...that's the last thing I remembered.

Chapter 50 -DEATH AND REBIRTH

The Void...Time passed without record. It may have been minutes, hours, or an eternity. I was lost in complete and utter emptiness. After an unknown passage of time, questions began to slowly emerge. Like a light in the darkness, consciousness began to form out of nothing. *What am I? Who am I?* My thoughts echoed through the darkness. I had self-awareness again.

Self-awareness formed out of emptiness. I was like a shadow in the night, blending with the Void, but I had my own identity; a spirit floating in the vastness of eternity. I was still forming and solidifying into what I was yet to become.

I began to be aware of physical reality. I became aware that I was "something" and I was "somewhere," but I could not tell who, what, or where. Substantial form took shape around me. I began to feel and use my body's senses.

I moved, slowly at first, a foot, then a leg, my arms. Gradually I became acquainted with my material body. I became more conscious of my senses and started to use them to figure out what and where I was. My eyes were now open, but the darkness around me was so complete, it didn't matter. There were no sounds except for my own breathing.

Crawling now, feeling my way upon the floor, I found that a wall encircled me. I continued crawling like an infant that didn't know how yet to stand. Then, using the wall for support, I managed to pull myself to my feet. Stumbling, my legs didn't want to hold that much weight, I groped about in the dark continuing to be propped up by the wall.

I searched; for what, I was not sure. As I stumbled around the circular room, I eventually found stairs cut into the earth, leading upward. I blindly began to find my way out of what now rang true as a pit. At the top of the stairs, I came to what seemed to be a doorway made of blankets. I shoved my arm through it and tossed the blankets back. My open eyes beheld a sight of awe and beauty, as if for the first time. Looking up, I saw the night sky, with the stars shining bright framed by the tops of pine trees.

As soon I saw the stars twinkling above, memories flooded back into my mind. I suddenly realized my purpose in being in that pit and what I was doing. I was on a Vision Quest, searching for the truth and the light. My life flashed before my eyes in an instant. I saw the life I had lived that brought me to this point.

I had just arisen from death, staring out into the starry night, cold, naked, and barely able to recall my own name. I stood reborn into this world.

I reentered the pit as soon as my memories returned.

The last day and night passed quickly. For the most part, I was still becoming aware and conscious of myself and who I was. Often I would just sit and beat my drum for hours. I heard a voice singing off in the distance, deep within the Earth. The voice would get louder and closer until I tried to hear it clearly, and then it would fade away. This went on for hours.

That night, I began to prepare myself to break the last remaining piercing. It was attached to my left chest. I waited until the darkness just before dawn before rising to my feet. As I stood, the walls of the pit faded away, and I was surrounded by empty space. Forms and shapes began to appear, flying and floating in from above me. The forms were that of humans, but I could not see anything distinguishable beyond the silhouettes of their heads, shoulders, and eyes. These "people" continued to enter the pit, until I was surrounded in a circle of rows upon rows, everyone looking at me.

They all stood there as if to watch me break this last piercing. I had the sense that they were my ancestors; grandfathers and grandmothers from ages. I felt honored that they would come to me in this way.

I knew this would be a difficult piercing to break. The flesh that held the pin to my chest had dried into a hard ribbon of hide. I strengthened myself mentally for what I had to do, and began to push myself backwards. I pulled against the rope with all my

Salvatore Gencarelle

strength, again and again. I braced myself so I would not fall against the spirits that were standing behind me. I pushed with my feet and pulled backwards with my chest. I pushed and pulled so hard and far that I was bent backwards.

Gritting my teeth, I gave one last tug, and the dried flesh gave away. My upper body flew backwards, colliding against the dirt wall of the pit. Earth crumbled and fell over my shoulders and head. The spirits were gone, and once again I was alone.

After breaking the last piercing, it was as if I had almost completely exited from the spirit world and returned back to the physical. I sat in peace and patiently waited to be brought from the pit to the sweat lodge. I said prayers of gratitude, saying my thanks for all that I had been given and all that was shown over the past days, and my lifetime.

It wasn't long before the blankets that covered the door were tossed aside and the morning light illuminated the darkness. Julie called to me from the doorway above. With my eyes still closed, I crawled from the pit and slowly walked to the sweat lodge. I felt stronger now than I had over the past few days, but I was still weak and dizzy. I was guided to the front of the lodge and crawled inside. Five hot stones were brought in one at a time. Cedar was offered to each of the stones and placed in the five directions. I sang the final offering song to the Grandfathers.

The Canupa was smoked and cleaned. The fire was extinguished, and the area was cleaned before we left the butte that morning.

We went to Wanblee, and I slept at Grandma Chipps' house. I awoke in the late afternoon and went to speak to Grandma about all that had happened. She translated the Lakota words that I had heard. When I explained all that I could about what took place, she looked at me in amazement. I was still too tired to realize everything that I had just experienced myself. It was going to take me years to process the past four days.

Prayer Song

> Do you hear the voice from above?
>
> If you do what this voice says you will walk in happiness.
>
> Do you hear the voice from above?
>
> If you do what this voice says you will live to stand with a cane.

CONCLUSION

Those nights of prayer, sacrifice, and seeking of wisdom on the butte forever changed my life. I touched the Void and was remade into something new, something more than what I had been just a few days before. In a sense, I died and was reborn. My old life faded away and I was infused with new life, transforming me from a Helper of ceremonies, to A Man Among the Helpers. I now walked in a new way with the guardians of the Earth and carried a Vision of hope for the future.

This book and the words that you have read are part of this Vision. This medicine and these spiritual ways must be passed on to the future generations, to ensure the survival of the human race. We all have been called to take responsibility for caretaking the Earth, our greatest gift, and to preserve life now and forever. Let us join together to right the wrong and bring balance back to the world, not for our own sake, but for our grandchildren's children.

It has now been over seven years since those nights of suffering and crying for a vision. Many things have changed, and many things have remained the same. Over the past years, I've returned to the dominant culture of America. I returned to learn more about American society, both the good and bad. This latest journey has given me a better understanding of the illnesses and the medical system of the modern age.

Every day I see how the old ways can be applied to our modern life, and how it would benefit people and all of creation. Over these past years, I've come to better understand my purpose for learning these sacred ways. I must help preserve these traditions for future generations, and do my part in bringing about true health and happiness for all of creation.

This book is just one part of my goal to bring these ancient ways back to all of humankind. Within this text is a template for those with the desire and heart to find their own Vision.

Offering Song

> *Come and see all of this*
>
> *Come and see all of this*
>
> *I offer all of this, pray with them for me*
>
> *I give you this, I will live*

ACKNOWLEDGMENTS:

I would first like to acknowledge and give thanks to all of creation that has supported me in this great adventure called life. My thanks goes out especially to the ancestors who have ensured that we have a world to be born into, that we have traditions that sustain us, and ceremonial methods to bring us back to balance when we have lost our way.

I would like to thank the modern day healers, Godfrey Chipps and Richard Moves Camp, for all their sacrifices so the people may live. Thanks to Andy Cooksey for introducing me to the Lakota. To Julie Chipps, who gave me three of the best sons a man could hope for. To Erica Thompson, who has given me a daughter to heal my heart, and her continuous love and support in writing this book. To all my family from Wanblee and the Reservation, I miss you all. To Jon Young and family in thanks for their support, guidance, and practical application of these traditions. Thank you to all who are named in this book, for your love and support through thick and thin.

Special thanks to Russ Reina, whose guidance and amazing ability to fuel the fires of creativity have been the driving force in the writing of this book.

CPSIA information can be obtained
at www.ICGtesting.com
Printed in the USA
FSOW02n1159020715
8490FS

9 781602 649392